AS IT WAS
IN THE DAYS
OF NOAH

AS IT WAS IN THE DAYS OF NOAH

A Wake-Up Call for Our Generation

David Hancox

As It Was in the Days of Noah
© 2025 David Hancox
All rights reserved.

ISBN: 9798289528599

Imprint: Independently published

First Edition: 2025

Cover Image © David Hancox

Contents

AS IT WAS
IN THE DAYS
OF NOAH

A Wake-Up Call for Our Generation

A bold wake-up call—exposing the signs of our times
through Matthew 24 and urging believers to live alert,
holy, and ready for Christ's return.

DEDICATION

To all who long for His return

"With heartfelt gratitude to the Divine—for the gift of wisdom, guidance, and presence throughout the creation of *As It Was in the Days of Noah*. Every word has been shaped by Your light, and this work stands as a reflection of Your boundless insight and grace."

To my beloved family, especially my cherished wife Tina, and our six remarkable children - James, Bradley, Thomas, Noah, Daisy, and Poppy - your unwavering support and love have been the cornerstone of my inspiration. Your patience during the countless hours spent writing is a testament to your understanding and belief in this endeavour.

To the congregation at Hope Church Oldbury, your encouragement has been a beacon of strength. Your faith and support have infused this work with a sense of purpose and determination, guiding me through moments of doubt.

May this offering, shaped by gratitude and love, resonate with those who encounter its pages, echoing the spirit of simplicity and depth.

I pray the lord will continue to bless you all,

Dave.

Introduction

We are living in a time of unprecedented global shaking—morally, spiritually, politically, and prophetically. Many in the Church have grown distracted, complacent, or unaware of the season we are in. This book is written as a **wake-up call** to believers everywhere: **time is short, Jesus is returning**, and we must be spiritually alert.

In *As It Was in the Days of Noah*, we will explore the words of Jesus in **Matthew 24**, His most direct and sobering teaching about the end times. We'll examine the signs He gave, the warnings He issued, and the urgent command to watch and be ready. Jesus did not speak in riddles—He gave us a roadmap, and it's unfolding before our very eyes.

We will also look at **the days of Noah**, a time Jesus said would mirror the generation alive at His return. What was society like in Noah's day? How does it compare to the world we see around us today? What does it mean to be righteous, prepared, and obedient in a corrupt and distracted age?

My prayer is that this book shakes you, stirs you, and awakens you to the **prophetic urgency of the hour**. It is time for the Church to rise, to return to holiness, to walk in truth, and to prepare for the soon coming of our King.

Let's open our hearts—and the Scriptures—and hear what the Spirit is saying to the Church.

Chapter 1

"The Questions That Shape the End"

"As Jesus was sitting on the Mount of Olives, the disciples came to him privately. 'Tell us,' they said, 'when will this happen, and what will be the sign of your coming and of the end of the age?'"

Matthew 24:3

The disciples here in this verse are curious— they're human, they are just like you and me.

They want to know the future. They're asking Jesus three things:

1. When will the Temple be destroyed?

2. What signs will show Jesus is coming back?

3. What signs will show the end of the world?

Today, we still ask these same questions. The only difference is that now we are asking: **when will the Temple be rebuilt?** This is often referred to as the **Third Temple.**

Several organisations are actively preparing for the potential rebuilding of the Temple:

The Temple Institute – Based in Jerusalem, this organisation has been dedicated to preparing for the construction of the Third Temple since its establishment in 1987. They have recreated over 90 ritual items, including priestly garments and sacred vessels, all intended for use in future Temple services. Additionally, they have trained a new generation of Levite priests and have been involved in identifying red heifers necessary for purification rituals.

Teams of architects and engineers have developed detailed plans for the Temple's design, drawing inspiration from biblical descriptions—particularly those found in the Book of Ezekiel. These plans aim to honour traditional interpretations while incorporating modern construction techniques.

The rebuilding of the Temple is essentially ready—we're just waiting for a start date!

Later in this book, we'll dive deeper into the rebuilding of the Third Temple and explore its profound implications for the world—especially as it sets the stage for the rise of the Antichrist.

Looking at our world today, we see a growing storm—**wars, natural disasters, global confusion**, and moral decline. It's no surprise that many are asking the same urgent question: **"Are we living in the end times?"**

Imagine you're sitting in a doctor's office and you hear the words: **"You're going to give birth soon."**

What's the first thing that comes to mind?

- If you're a man, you'd probably say, **"Whatttt?!"**

- If you're a woman, the immediate questions would be: **"When?"** and **"What signs should I look out for?"**

That's exactly what the disciples asked Jesus.

They weren't confused about the fact that something big was coming. They wanted to know:

When will it happen?
What signs should we be watching for?

These are the same questions we'll be exploring as we **go through Matthew 24**—Jesus' most powerful teaching on the signs of the times.

Chapter 2

"Deception, Division, and Endurance"

"Jesus answered: 'Watch out that no one deceives you.'" — Matthew 24:4

Beware of Deception

Before anything else, Jesus warned them:
"Be careful—don't be fooled."

Deception will come first.
False teachers. Fake saviours. Misleading messages.

Today, **social media is flooded with spiritual "influencers."**
Some preach the truth—others twist it.

Just because someone is popular doesn't mean they speak for God.

Be **very careful** what you watch online and on so-called *Christian TV channels.*
Especially when someone asks you to part with your money in exchange for an "anointed

15

handkerchief" and promises that, once received, it will bring you **prosperity and healing**.

Listen carefully, child of God—
The Word of God tells us that **the same power that raised Christ from the dead lives in you** (Romans 8:11).

You must put your faith in **God and His Word—**
not in some flashy TV preacher.
Amen.

A Warning from Scripture

2 Timothy 4:3 (NIV)
"For the time will come when people will not put up with sound doctrine. Instead, to suit their own desires, they will gather around them a great number of teachers to say what their itching ears want to hear."

The Modern Pulpit Crisis

Sadly, much of what is preached in churches today has been reduced to **motivational talks** or **life-coaching sessions**—void of any mention of **sin, repentance, hell,** or the **soon return of Jesus Christ.**

It's time to return to preaching **the full truth of the Gospel**, no matter how uncomfortable it may be—
Because **only the truth can set people free.**

Deception by False Messiahs

"For many will come in my name, claiming, 'I am the Messiah,' and will deceive many."
— Matthew 24:5

Explanation

Jesus warns that in the last days, many will come pretending to speak for Him—or even claim to be Him. They will draw people away from the truth, leading them into deception. These individuals may appear persuasive, even spiritual, but they do not represent the true Messiah.
False teaching always wears a mask of truth.

17

Have you ever seen a counterfeit £20 note? It may look and feel real—but it's worthless.

That's exactly what false messiahs and deceivers are like: convincing on the outside, but completely void of the power and truth of Christ.

Modern-Day Examples of False Messiahs

- **David Koresh** led the Branch Davidians in Waco, Texas, claiming to be the final prophet. His teachings ended in a siege and tragic fire, killing dozens.

- **Jim Jones**, founder of the People's Temple, convinced over 900 followers to commit mass suicide in Jonestown, Guyana. He claimed divine status and manipulated scripture for personal control.

- **Sun Myung Moon**, founder of the Unification Church, declared himself the Messiah and misled countless followers through a distorted gospel.

These are not just historical tragedies—they are stark **warnings** of how easily people can be deceived when they abandon the Word of God for **charisma and claims**.

The Need for Discernment

We are living in times when spiritual deception is on the rise. Social media, self-proclaimed prophets, and pseudo-Christian movements are becoming increasingly bold.
As believers, we must test everything against **the Word of God** (1 John 4:1).

If it doesn't align with Scripture—it's not from God.

Jesus was clear: many will come *in His name* but will lead **many** astray.
Let's make sure we are not among them.

Wars and Rumours of Wars

"You will hear of wars and rumours of wars, but see to it that you are not alarmed. Such things must happen, but the end is still to come."
— *Matthew 24:6*

Jesus warned that wars and escalating conflict would characterise the days leading up to His return.

From ancient times to the present, conflict has been a **recurring theme in human history**. But Christ's words remind us: **these things must happen**, and we must not be shaken or live in fear.

Past and Present: A Pattern of War

History bears witness to the truth of Jesus' words.
In the last century alone:

- **World War I (1914–1918)** devastated nations and introduced warfare on a global scale.

- **World War II (1939–1945)** brought genocide, global destruction, and the use of atomic bombs.

- The **Cold War** created a world gripped by fear of nuclear annihilation.

- The **Gulf War**, **9/11**, and the **War on Terror** reshaped geopolitics and religious conflict.

These were not isolated incidents—they were part of a growing, global pattern of unrest that continues to this day.

Today's Comparison

We are living in the fulfilment of this prophecy.

- The **ongoing war between Russia and Ukraine** has shaken Europe and impacted the global economy.

- In the **Middle East**, tensions have dangerously escalated between **Israel and Iran**, with open threats of war and international concern.

- Other regions are marked by **civil unrest, coups, terrorism, and political instability**.

These events are deeply troubling—but they are not random. They are signs that Jesus told us to expect.

A Call to Spiritual Focus

While the world spirals in chaos, the believer is called to remain **anchored in Christ**.
Jesus didn't share these prophecies to frighten us —but to prepare us.
"Do not be alarmed." He remains sovereign over history.

Let these signs not drive us to fear—but to **faith**, **watchfulness**, and a renewed urgency to proclaim the Gospel.

Famines, Earthquakes, and a Groaning Earth

"Nation will rise against nation, and kingdom against kingdom. There will be famines and earthquakes in various places."
— *Matthew 24:7*

Jesus foretold a time when **conflict, famine, and natural disasters** would multiply across the earth. Not only would nations clash, but **the planet itself would groan** under the weight of sin and suffering.

These are not isolated events. They're part of a **clear prophetic pattern**—and we are witnessing it unfold in real time.

Modern-Day Earthquakes

1. **Myanmar – 28 March 2025**
   A powerful 7.7-magnitude earthquake struck central Myanmar, followed by a 6.4 aftershock and several smaller tremors.
   At least **144 people died**, over **700 were injured**, and homes, religious sites, and heritage structures were destroyed. The military junta declared a **state of emergency** and requested international aid.
   (Source: Wall Street Journal)

2. **Istanbul, Turkey – 23 April 2025**
   A 6.2-magnitude quake caused widespread panic in Turkey's largest city. Over **150 injuries** occurred as residents fled buildings.
   More than **50 aftershocks** followed, including one at 5.9 magnitude. Although no deaths were reported, the quake raised alarm—**1.5 million buildings** remain at

risk in the city.
(Sources: Financial Times, Irish Sun, Reuters)

3. New Zealand – 30 April 2025

Two significant quakes struck offshore: one at 6.2 magnitude near Invercargill, and a stronger 6.8 near the Macquarie Islands.

Thankfully, there were **no reports of damage** or tsunami warnings.

(Sources: AP, USGS)

4. Alaska, USA – April 2025

Mount Spurr, an active volcano near Anchorage, recorded **22 earthquakes** in April.

While initial data suggested a potential eruption, recent analysis shows a **decline in activity**, reducing the immediate risk.

(Source: New York Post)

Global Earthquake Statistics *(as of April 2025 – USGS)*

- 4 earthquakes of **magnitude 7.0 or higher**

- 32 between **6.0 and 7.0**

- 537 between **5.0 and 6.0**

Famines and Food Insecurity

- **Sudan**: Ongoing civil war has caused famine-like conditions. Over **500,000 children** have died from malnutrition.

- **Haiti**: Gang violence has driven **nearly half the population** into famine, with **5.4 million people** suffering acute food insecurity.

- **Global**: In 2023, a record **281 million people** across 59 countries faced **acute hunger**—the highest figure ever recorded.

These aren't just numbers. They are the **lived reality** of suffering humanity. And they are exactly what Jesus said would happen.

Romans 8:22 – *"We know that the whole creation has been groaning as in the pains of childbirth."*

The Beginning of Birth Pains

"All these are the beginning of birth pains."
— *Matthew 24:8*

Jesus makes it clear: the wars, famines, earthquakes, and global unrest are not the end—but just the beginning.

Just like labour pains signal that **something is about to be born**, these prophetic signs are spiritual contractions—**growing closer together, stronger, and more intense** as the moment approaches.

When a mother goes into labour, the pain is real —**but it's not pointless**. It means something is about to happen. Something beautiful. A birth.

Likewise, the upheaval we see in the world today is painful—but it is not meaningless. It points to something greater: **the coming of Christ's Kingdom**, the return of our King.

Each wave of suffering, each global crisis, each natural disaster is a reminder that the clock is ticking and the promises of God are drawing nearer.

We mustn't panic—we must **prepare**.

"The labour pains have begun. The Church must be awake, alert, and ready—because the delivery is closer than we think."

Chapter 3

"Faith Under Fire"

Persecuted for His Name

"Then you will be handed over to be persecuted and put to death, and you will be hated by all nations because of me."
— *Matthew 24:9*

Jesus didn't promise comfort—He warned of **persecution**.

His followers would be hated, targeted, imprisoned, even killed—not for doing wrong, but for standing for **truth**.

This isn't just history. It's **happening now**.

Modern-Day Persecution

- **North Korea & China**: Christians are monitored, arrested, and tortured for gathering in secret or owning a Bible.

- **Nigeria (April 2025)**: Over **150 Christians were killed** in brutal rural violence. Peaceful farming villages were attacked—often targeted in ongoing clashes between **nomadic Muslim herders and Christian communities.**

- **Global Trends**: In many countries, believers face **discrimination, imprisonment, violence, and execution** for their faith in Christ.

John 15:18 – *"If the world hates you, keep in mind that it hated me first."*

What About the West?

Persecution in the West may not look the same, but it is very real:

- **Silent prayer arrests** near abortion clinics in the UK have sparked serious concern over freedom of belief.

- **Job losses** and disciplinary action for expressing **traditional Christian views** —especially on marriage and gender—are becoming more common.

- **Attacks on churches**: Reports show **over 4,000 incidents** involving Christian places of worship in the UK alone—ranging from hate crimes to vandalism and theft.

Despite the media narrative that **"Islam is a religion of peace,"** tell that to the **Christian families in Nigeria** mourning loved ones killed for their faith.

The Cost of Following Jesus

Persecution is not just a prophecy—it's a **present reality**. And yet, Jesus reminds us:

"Blessed are those who are persecuted because of righteousness, for theirs is the kingdom of heaven."(Matthew 5:10)

The Great Falling Away

"At that time many will turn away from the faith and will betray and hate each other."
— *Matthew 24:10*

This verse is a **sobering warning** from Jesus Himself.

In the last days, many will **"turn away"**—the Greek word used here is *skandalizō* (scan-de-lees-o), meaning to stumble, fall into sin, or **abandon truth** due to offence, pressure, or fear.

And these aren't just people who never knew God. These are **former believers**—those who once sat in pews, lifted their hands in worship, served in ministry, and professed faith in Christ.

But when **persecution intensifies**, when **truth becomes costly**, and when **culture clashes with Scripture**, they will **walk away**.

Worse still, some won't just leave quietly—they'll **betray** fellow believers, **criticise**, and even **oppose the truth** they once embraced.

This isn't just doubt—it's **disloyalty, division, and deep deception**.

Today's Comparison

Just look around.

- Churches are **splitting over secondary issues.**

- Christians argue over politics, race, gender, masks, and vaccines—sometimes more **passionately than they defend the Gospel.**

- Social media has become a battlefield of believers **tearing each other down** over doctrine, denominations, or opinions.

- Many now choose **culture over Christ**, trading conviction for comfort and approval.

Denominations in Compromise

Some major denominations—under pressure from secular society—have **compromised the Word of God:**

- Certain Anglican, Methodist, and Presbyterian groups have begun **blessing same-sex marriages**, despite clear biblical teaching.

- Others now **deny the reality of hell**, or **reinterpret Scripture** to avoid offending modern audiences.

- In some churches, **sin is never mentioned**, and repentance is replaced by self-help.

Rather than lovingly uphold the truth, they've chosen **popularity over purity**, and **inclusivity over integrity**.

"For the time will come when people will not put up with sound doctrine. Instead, to suit their own desires, they will gather around them a great number of teachers to say what their itching ears want to hear."
— *2 Timothy 4:3*

Choose Conviction Over Compromise

Jesus **warned us**: Truth will become unpopular. The cost of discipleship will rise. But in that moment, the true Church must **stand firm**—united, unashamed, and unmovable.

"He who stands firm to the end will be saved." (Matthew 24:13)

Deception in the Pulpit

"And many false prophets will appear and deceive many people."
— Matthew 24:11

Jesus didn't say *some*—He said **many** false prophets will rise.

These individuals will **claim to speak for God**, yet **distort truth**, often motivated by **money, fame, or power**.

They will appear convincing. Many will be eloquent, charismatic, even popular. But behind the smile and polished sermons lies a **false message**, stripped of the Gospel and anchored in self-interest.

1 John 4:1 — *"Dear friends, do not believe every spirit, but test the spirits to see whether they are from God, because many false prophets have gone out into the world."*

Modern Forms of Deception

Prosperity Preachers

"Send your seed—receive your miracle!"
They promise health, wealth, and breakthrough in exchange for your money, yet **never mention holiness, repentance, or sacrifice**. The cross becomes a stepping stone to personal success rather than a call to die to self.

Churchtainment

Worship has, in some places, become **a concert, not a consecration**.
Loud music, flashing lights, fog machines—and yet no **fear of the Lord**.
People come to be **entertained, not transformed**.
The service is slick, the band is tight, the atmosphere is electric—but **the presence of God is absent**.
Emotions are stirred, but hearts are not changed.
Church was never meant to be a performance—it's a place of reverence, repentance, and encounter with the living God.

Celebrity Pastors

Popular, relevant, and media-savvy. But often, the message is **watered down**.
"Positive vibes" take the place of preaching on

sin, judgment, or the return of Christ.
They fear offending man more than offending
God.

Cult Leaders & Mystics

From **Jim Jones** to **David Koresh**, history
shows us the tragic results when **control,
charisma, and deception** collide.
Today, we see a similar pattern in "prophets" who
exploit spiritual hunger for personal gain, leading
people into legalism, control, or spiritual abuse.

Why This Warning Matters

Deception today doesn't always shout—it
whispers in Christian language.
It hides behind **well-edited sermons, slick
graphics, and feel-good messages**.
Jesus warned us in Matthew 7 that **wolves will
come in sheep's clothing**—meaning the
danger is not obvious.

That's why now, more than ever, we must return
to the **Word of God** as our standard, not what's
popular or exciting.

Discernment Is Critical

"The Bereans... examined the Scriptures daily to see if what Paul said was true." — *Acts 17:11*

If even Paul's words were tested, so should every message we hear today.
If a preacher downplays repentance, ignores holiness, or avoids the Cross—**walk away**.
Truth might be uncomfortable—but only truth **sets people free**.

Hearts Gone Cold

"Because of the increase of wickedness, the love of most will grow cold."
— Matthew 24:12

Sin will spread.
Hearts will harden.
People will become **numb**—no compassion, no conviction, no care.

Like a fire that dies when it's no longer fed, **love fades** when we stop nourishing it.

When sin is allowed to reign unchecked in our lives and societies, **love withers.**

Today's Signs:

- **Online bullying** and vicious comment sections filled with hatred.

- **Road rage** turning into violent assaults.

- **School shootings** and youth violence becoming tragically "normal."

- Even many **Christians** seem weary, disconnected, or indifferent—no longer moved by what breaks God's heart.

Never before in history have we seen so many **children involved in murder and violent crime.**
Knife crime is at an all-time high, particularly in urban areas of the UK.
What once shocked us now barely stirs emotion.

We've become desensitised.
As sin increases, **compassion decreases.**
When wickedness becomes normalised, the warmth of love is replaced with **cold-hearted apathy.**

Warning for the Church: A Wake-Up Call

Let's be honest—something is desperately wrong in the Church.

This isn't just a societal issue—it's a **spiritual issue**.

Even within churches, people can lose their first love (Revelation 2:4).

Worship becomes routine. Prayer becomes rare. The fire of faith flickers out.

The least attended service in most churches is the prayer meeting.

That's not just disappointing—it's **alarming**.

We say we want revival.

We say we want to see God move.

We say we want change in our homes, our cities, and our nation...

But we can't even be bothered to show up and pray?

Prayer is not a side dish—it's the **main course**.

It's not optional. It's **critical**.

We're not in a tea party—we're in a **war**, and our

greatest weapon is being left on the shelf collecting dust.

This is not a time for passive Christianity.
It's time to **wake up**, fall on our knees, and get back in the fight.
You can't win a spiritual battle with your hands in your pockets.
You win it on your **knees**—in the secret place, in the prayer room, in desperate intercession before God.

2 Chronicles 7:14 – *"If my people, who are called by my name, will humble themselves and pray... then I will hear from heaven..."*

Church—**PRAY.**
Not when it's convenient.
Not when it fits into your schedule.
Now. Urgently. With fire.

"Prayer isn't preparation for the battle—**prayer IS the battle.**" – Leonard Ravenhil

Pray With Me

Father God,
We come before You humbled and broken.
We see the darkness rising, the wickedness

increasing, and the love of many growing cold —
and we confess, Lord... **we've been asleep**.
We've become distracted, disconnected, and too
comfortable.
We've let the fire die down.

Forgive us for trading prayer for convenience.
Forgive us for treating the place of intercession
like an optional extra instead of our **lifeline**.
Forgive us for allowing the world to influence us
more than Your Word.

Lord, awaken our hearts again.
Set a fire in us that cannot be quenched.
Stir a hunger to seek Your face—not just on
Sundays, not just when things go wrong, but
every day, with urgency and passion.

We don't want to be a Church that talks about
revival—we want to **birth revival** through
prayer, repentance, and obedience.
Raise up warriors. Raise up a Church that prays
like lives depend on it—because they do.

Let the cry of our hearts be:
**"Not my will, but Yours be done. On our
knees, in Your power, for Your glory."In
Jesus' mighty name,
Amen.**

Chapter 4

"Endurance and the End of the Age"

"But the one who stands firm to the end will be saved." – Matthew 24:13

This is not a throwaway verse.
This is Jesus **sounding the rallying cry** in the midst of chaos, persecution, and deception.
This is **hope wrapped in a command**: *Stand firm. Endure. Hold the line.*

We are not called to be spectators—we are called to be **soldiers**.
We are not called to retreat—we are called to **stand**.

The enemy is fierce. The pressure is real. The culture is hostile.
But if you **stand firm**, Jesus promises—you *will be saved*.

This is not about perfection. It's about perseverance.

You may stumble. You may struggle. You may weep.
But God doesn't call the flawless—He calls the **faithful**.

2 Timothy 2:12 – "If we endure, we will also reign with Him."

He's not looking for superstars.
He's looking for those who **won't quit** when the fire gets hot.

Modern-Day Example: North Korean Christians

Right now, in North Korea, Christians meet in **secret basements**, whispering songs of worship because to be caught with a Bible could mean death—or worse.
And yet—they gather. They pray. They endure.

Why?
Because they know the truth is worth more than their comfort.
Because they believe that what waits at the end is greater than what they suffer now.

That's endurance.

They are the living, breathing fulfilment of Matthew 24:13—**standing firm when it costs them everything.**

Illustration: The Marathon Mindset

Think of a marathon runner.
The road is long. There are moments of agony.
Cramp. Exhaustion. Temptation to stop.

But there's something that keeps them going:
The finish line.

They don't run because it's easy—they run because they know it's worth it.

That's the Christian life.
Some days you'll feel like sprinting. Other days, you'll barely crawl.
But if you *don't quit*—you finish. And if you finish—you win.

Church, Hear This Loud and Clear

We are living in a time where comfort is idolised and commitment is rare.
The modern church has been seduced by convenience.

But Jesus didn't promise ease—He promised eternal reward.

If you're going to stand firm in this hour, you will need:

- A **backbone**, not just a wishbone.

- **Grit**, not just good feelings.

- A heart that's **anchored in truth**, not blown about by trends.

Keep your armour on.

Keep your fire lit.

Keep your knees bent in prayer.

Keep your Bible open.

Keep moving forward—even if it's just one faithful step at a time.

Because the one who stands firm to the end **will** be saved.

"And this gospel of the kingdom will be preached in the whole world as a testimony to all nations, and then the end will come." – Matthew 24:14

Before the end comes, the **Good News** of the Kingdom must be proclaimed to **every tribe, tongue, and nation**. This is not a suggestion—it is a divine mandate and a prophetic certainty.

Modern Progress:

We are witnessing this unfold in our time.

- **Internet and Technology:**
  Thanks to digital innovation—smartphones, satellite TV, YouTube, podcasts, and livestreams—the Gospel is now accessible in the most remote corners of the earth. People in closed nations, war zones, or isolated communities are hearing the name of Jesus for the first time.

- **Global Missions:**
  Brave men and women still answer the call to go. Missionaries are on the front lines—walking jungle paths, sailing rivers, crossing deserts—bringing the light of Christ into spiritual darkness.

- **Bible Translation:**
  Ministries like Wycliffe and others are working tirelessly to translate the Bible into every language, so all may hear God speak in their own tongue.

- **Social Media & Online Platforms:**
  Millions are engaging with the Gospel daily through online devotionals, Christian influencers, virtual churches, and digital Bibles. The digital pulpit is global, and it's thriving.

All of these efforts are fulfilling what Jesus declared: *the Gospel would go to the ends of the earth before the end comes.*

Revelation 7:9 reminds us of what's coming:

"A great multitude that no one could count, from every nation, tribe, people and language, standing before the throne and before the Lamb..."

That vision is not a fantasy—it's a future reality. And you, child of God, are part of the generation helping to bring it to pass.

So, don't be discouraged by the darkness in the world. Be motivated by the light of this promise: **we are on mission**, and God's word will not return void.

Reflection: Standing Firm and Spreading the Gospel

Jesus doesn't sugar-coat the reality: the days ahead will be tough. Hearts will grow cold, truth will be unpopular, persecution will rise. But those who **endure**, who hold tightly to their faith despite the pressure, **will be saved**. God honours the faithful. He sees those who keep going when others give up, those who choose righteousness over comfort, and truth over trend.

But Jesus also lifts our eyes beyond the chaos.

The mission is still moving forward. The **Gospel is not losing**—it's advancing.

Even in dark times, the Good News is **shining brighter** than ever. Technology, missions, and divine boldness are opening doors across continents. God is orchestrating a global awakening—souls are being saved, churches are being planted, and the message of Jesus is being

47

proclaimed in **languages that had never heard His name** before.

This is both a **call to persevere** and a **call to participate**.

Are you standing firm? Are you sharing the Gospel? Are you part of the great mission Jesus spoke of?

This isn't the time to shrink back. This is the time to rise up—with boldness, with faith, with urgency. The finish line is getting closer. Let us run with endurance and preach with passion, knowing that **we are the generation helping to complete the mission** Jesus began.

Will You Stand?

Take a moment and ask yourself honestly:

- Am I standing firm—or sliding into silence?

- Is my faith built on **feeling**, or is it rooted in **truth**?

- When pressure comes, will I **follow the crowd**, or will I **stand for Christ**?

The road ahead is not easy. Jesus made that clear. But He also made this clear: **those who endure will be saved**.
Not those who blend in.
Not those who bow to culture.
Not those who give up when it's hard.

But those who keep going—who cling to Christ when everything else shakes.

This is not about fear.
This is about **faithfulness**.
You were not born for easy days—you were born for *such a time as this*.

Let this chapter be a call to rise—not in your own strength, but in the power of the Holy Spirit.

Decide now: No matter what comes, *I will stand firm*.
Not because I'm strong—but because **He who called me is faithful**.

1 Corinthians 16:13
"Be on your guard; stand firm in the faith; be courageous; be strong."

Ephesians 6:13

"Therefore put on the full armour of God, so that when the day of evil comes, you may be able to stand your ground, and after you have done everything, to stand."

1 Peter 5:9

"Resist him, standing firm in the faith, because you know that the family of believers throughout the world is undergoing the same kind of sufferings."

Revelation 3:11

"I am coming soon. Hold on to what you have, so that no one will take your crown."

Chapter 5

"The Abomination in the Holy Place"

"So when you see standing in the holy place 'the abomination that causes desolation,' spoken of through the prophet Daniel—let the reader understand" – Matthew 24:15

What Does This Really Mean?

Jesus isn't speaking metaphorically here.

He's giving *specific, prophetic intelligence* to future believers—those who will live to see the unthinkable: a moment when the sacred centre of worship is hijacked by satanic power.

Prophetic Revelation

The "holy place" refers to the rebuilt **Jewish Temple in Jerusalem**—a physical location of worship that will exist during the **Tribulation period**.

The "abomination of desolation" is more than a statue or a political stunt.

It is the ultimate betrayal of God:

A man, **empowered by Satan**, stepping into God's house, declaring himself to be God, and demanding worship from all humanity.

Cross References

- **Daniel 9:27** – "…in the middle of the 'seven' he will put an end to sacrifice and offering."

- **2 Thessalonians 2:4** – "He sets himself up in God's temple, proclaiming himself to be God."

- **Revelation 13:15** – The image of the beast is given breath and forces all to worship—under penalty of death.

Jesus Is Warning Us

The day is coming when **evil won't just whisper from dark corners—**
it will **march into God's house**, sit on His throne, and dare to say:

"I am God."

That's not just a **bad day**—
It's the **final insult** before judgment falls.

Jesus doesn't say "if" but **"when"** this happens.
And then He adds:
"Let the reader understand."
In other words:
Don't skim this. Don't spiritualise it. Don't ignore
it.
Grasp it. Feel it. Prepare for it.

This isn't abstract theology—it's *strategic
prophecy.*

Why This Is the Final Insult to God

Throughout Scripture, God's dwelling place—
whether the **Tabernacle, Solomon's Temple**,
or even the **heart of a believer**—is sacred.
It's where **heaven touches earth**. Where **truth
is proclaimed** and **sins are atoned**.

But here?
A **counterfeit messiah** enters the Holy of
Holies and sits where only God belongs.

Imagine this:

A stranger breaks into your home.
He sits in your seat at the table.
Puts on your clothes.
And tells your children:
"I'm your father now. Obey me."

That's what the **Antichrist** will do in God's house.
And God will not tolerate it.

We already live in a world *primed for deception*:

- **Digital ID systems** being developed to control buying and selling.

- **AI avatars** that mimic spiritual figures and speak "revelations."

- **Global unity movements**, pushing for a **universal religion** in the name of peace.

- A generation trained to value **image over truth**, **feeling over faith**, and **tolerance over holiness**.

Now picture this:

A charismatic **global leader** emerges.
He brokers a 7 year peace deal in the Middle East, solves world hunger through biotech, unites nations under a digital currency.

He walks into the rebuilt Temple.
The entire world watches on livestream.
He announces:

"I am the embodiment of all gods.
Worship me. Follow me.
Reject me—and you'll lose everything."

Celebrities endorse him.
Tech companies promote his image.
World leaders bow.
And the world kneels.

That's not **science fiction**.
That's **biblical prophecy**—and the stage is being set *right now*.

"Then let those who are in Judea flee to the mountains. Let no one on the housetop go down to take anything out of the house. Let no one in the field go back to get their cloak."
– Matthew 24:16-18

When the Sign Appears: Run, Don't Hesitate

Jesus isn't speaking figuratively—He's giving life-saving instructions.
When that sign appears, don't try to fix things, don't argue, don't protest.
Run.

"If you're nearby, don't wait—get out fast!"

Think of it like an emergency alert—whether it's a storm warning, a wildfire evacuation, or an air raid siren.
The time to move is **immediately**.
Not after you've grabbed your phone.
Not after you've gathered your valuables.
Now.

Hesitation Could Be Fatal

Jesus is emphasising **urgency.**

"Don't go back to grab your phone, your wallet, or even your jacket.
Your life is more important than your stuff."

In wildfires, people have lost their lives trying to rescue pets, retrieve photos, or grab heirlooms.
Jesus is making the same point here:
Don't let anything—no possession, no priority, no second thought—slow you down when God says move.

This Is Not the Time to Cling to Earthly Things

This is a warning for us too.

When the world is falling apart, when the signs become undeniable, when the call to flee or obey comes—it's not the time to be *clutching the temporary.*

Your security isn't in your possessions.
Your identity isn't in your home.
Your salvation isn't in anything you can carry.

What matters is **obedience**.
What matters is **faith**.
What matters is **life**.

"How dreadful it will be in those days for pregnant women and nursing mothers! Pray that your flight will not take place in winter or on the Sabbath."– Matthew 24:19-20

A Time of Unimaginable Hardship

Jesus acknowledges something deeply human: **Not everyone will be in the same condition when trouble comes.**

For pregnant women, nursing mothers, the elderly, and the physically vulnerable, the coming tribulation will be especially severe.

In plain terms:

"It's going to be even harder for those already carrying a heavy load."

Real-World Comparison

Think of **refugees fleeing war-zones**—mothers with babies in their arms, walking miles in freezing weather, with no food, shelter, or medical care.
That's the level of hardship Jesus is warning about.

And it's not just about physical struggle—**timing matters too**:

- **Winter** brings cold, danger, and slower travel.

- **The Sabbath** (especially in Jewish culture) restricts movement and access to resources.

Jesus urges His followers to **pray**—not just to survive, but to **avoid extra obstacles** if possible.

"Pray that when the moment comes, you're not burdened by added hardship."

"Pray your path to safety isn't blocked by freezing weather, cultural restrictions, or personal limitations."

A Message of Compassion and Preparation

This verse isn't just about warning—it's full of **compassion**. Jesus sees those who suffer most. He doesn't overlook the vulnerable.

It's also a call to **spiritual alertness**:
Start praying now—not just for strength to endure, but for mercy in the timing.

It's like needing to evacuate your home during a blizzard—or when the trains are shut down.

Jesus is saying: **"Pray you'll be able to escape easily when the time comes."**

"For then there will be great distress, unequalled from the beginning of the world until now—and never to be equalled again. If those days had not been cut short, no one would survive, but for the sake of the elect those days will be shortened."– Matthew 24:19-20

A Time Like No Other

This is not just any period of hardship. Jesus is describing a time of **unprecedented suffering—greater than anything the world has ever known**, or will ever know again.

"This will be the worst crisis in human history."

Think of History's Greatest Tragedies:

- Two **World Wars**

- The **Holocaust**

- **Global pandemics**

- **Natural disasters** that left nations in ruins

As horrific as those were, Jesus says **they don't even come close** to what's coming during the **Great Tribulation**.

This is **humanity at its darkest**, and yet—it won't last forever.

God's Mercy in the Midst of Judgment

"If those days had not been cut short, no one would survive..."

The devastation will be so severe that **total annihilation** would be inevitable—**unless God intervenes**.

But He will.

"...but for the sake of the elect, those days will be shortened."

A Powerful Truth

God will not abandon His people.

Just as a **war might be ended by a peace treaty**, or a **pandemic halted by a breakthrough**,
God Himself will step in—**not because the world deserves it**, but **because His people are still here**.

For the sake of the elect—those who remain faithful—**God will limit the destruction**.

Hold on. Stay faithful. The storm will rage—but it will not last forever.

Chapter 6

"The Age of Deception"

"At that time if anyone says to you, 'Look, here is the Messiah!' or, 'There he is!' do not believe it."– Matthew 24:23

Deception Will Run Wild

Jesus gives a **clear and urgent warning**:
In the chaos of the end times, many **false saviours**, **self-proclaimed messiahs**, and **spiritual frauds** will rise up.
They will claim to be Him—or claim to speak on His behalf.

"Don't believe it," Jesus says. "Don't fall for the noise."

This is not just a spiritual footnote—**it's a survival warning.**

The Danger of Being Spiritually Gullible

We live in a world **saturated with self-proclaimed prophets**:

- Cult leaders who claim divine authority

- Internet influencers preaching a false gospel

- YouTubers and TikTok personalities claiming special revelation

- Individuals who twist Scripture to fit their personal agendas

They gather followers not because they preach truth, but because **they say what itching ears want to hear** (2 Timothy 4:3).

Some promise peace.
Some offer power.
Some claim to have secret knowledge or "new truth."

But **Jesus says clearly**:

"Do not believe them."

What's the Safeguard?

Discernment.

How do we avoid being deceived?

By staying **anchored in God's Word**.

Know the real, and you'll spot the counterfeit.

Bankers aren't trained by studying fake notes—they're trained by handling the real ones every day.
Likewise, Christians must stay grounded in **biblical truth**, so that when deception comes, **we immediately sense it doesn't line up** with what we know to be true.

Stand Guard Over Your Heart

In uncertain times, people become desperate for hope, for answers, for security.
That's when **false messiahs thrive**—offering what seems to be the light but is actually darkness in disguise.

"Trust no substitute. Wait for the real Christ."

When Jesus returns, **there will be no doubt**.

It won't be a livestream. It won't be a secret gathering.
It will be **undeniable, glorious, and universal**.

Jesus doesn't just predict deception—**He arms us against it**.
Stay sharp. Stay rooted. Don't chase every spiritual trend or voice.

If someone has to convince you they're the Messiah, **they're not**.

"For false messiahs and false prophets will appear and perform great signs and wonders to deceive, if possible, even the elect."– Matthew 24:24

Deception with Power

Jesus isn't talking about simple tricksters—He warns that **false messiahs and prophets** will come with **real displays of power**.
Miraculous signs. Wonders. Supernatural acts.

These aren't party magicians—they will seem spiritual, convincing, and even impressive.

Their goal? **To deceive**—to lead people away from the truth.
Even the elect—true believers—could be at risk, if not spiritually anchored.

Signs and Wonders ≠ Truth

Not every miracle is from God.
The **enemy can mimic signs** to confuse and mislead.

These false prophets will appear **credible**, even "anointed."
But their power isn't from Heaven—it's a counterfeit designed to lead people astray.

Modern Parallels: Deception is Evolving

Think of today's technology:

- **Deepfake videos** that imitate real people

- **AI-generated images** and voices that sound authentic

- **Digitally altered content** so realistic it's hard to tell what's true

They look real—but they're fake.

Spiritual deception works the same way.
It feels right. Sounds right. Looks right. But it's wrong.

If you rely on feelings or appearances, you'll be misled.
Only the Word of God and the Holy Spirit can keep you grounded in truth.

Stay Rooted in Truth

The only way to avoid being deceived is to know the real Jesus intimately.

This is why **biblical literacy** matters.
This is why **daily prayer** matters.
This is why **being filled with the Holy Spirit** matters.

We live in an age where **truth is under attack** —

Not just intellectually, but **spiritually**.

False prophets won't look evil.
They may be charming, persuasive, even "miraculous."
But Jesus says: **Don't be fooled.**

If it doesn't line up with the Gospel, with Scripture, and with the Spirit of Christ—reject it.

"See, I have told you ahead of time." – Matthew 24:25

Jesus is saying, **"I'm giving you this warning now so you're not caught off guard."**

"I'm telling you now so you can be ready later."

Like a teacher who gives a heads-up about a coming exam, Jesus isn't trying to frighten us— He's preparing His followers in advance.
Not to scare. To protect.

How Should We Respond Today?

WHAT SHOULD WE DO?

1. Be Watchful, Not Fearful

Jesus didn't share this prophecy to **paralyse** us —but to **prepare** us.

"Let the reader understand."

This is a call to **biblical literacy**.
Don't just skim over prophecy—**study it. Know it. Teach it.**
Be alert. Stay sharp. We're meant to be people of discernment, not panic.

2. Anchor Yourself in Truth

The deception coming will be so strong, **even the elect**—committed believers—could be **tempted to fall for it**.

"If possible, even the elect would be deceived." – *Matthew 24:24*

Now is the time to be **deeply grounded** in the Word of God.
Your foundation must be so solid in Christ that **no lie can shake you**.

Don't rely on social media prophets or trending theology.
Return to the Scriptures. Be led by the Spirit, not the spotlight.
Let your faith be built on rock, not sand.

Sound the Alarm

Warn your family.
Warn your church.
Warn your generation.

This is not **conspiracy theory**—
This is **biblical clarity**.
Speak the truth **in love**,
but **do not stay silent**.

A Final Word of Victory

Yes, the Antichrist will rise.
Yes, he will **stand in the holy place**.
Yes, he will **desecrate what is sacred**.
Yes, he will **deceive millions**.

But **he will not reign forever**.

There is **another coming**:

Jesus Christ – the **true King**, the **Lion of Judah**, the **Lamb of God**.

He will return—**not to be questioned or resisted**,

but to **overthrow evil**, **cleanse the holy place**, and **reign in righteousness**.

Until Then...

Stay alert, Stay faithful, Stay awake!

Don't be caught sleeping when the world needs a Church that's wide awake.

Chapter 7

Don't Be Deceived — The Signs Before the Sign

"So if anyone tells you, 'There he is, out in the wilderness,' do not go out; or, 'Here he is, in the inner rooms,' do not believe it." – Matthew 24:26

Jesus is warning His followers **not to fall for false messiahs or sensational claims**.

Some will say, "He's out in the wilderness!" or "He's hidden in a private room!"
But Jesus says clearly: **Don't believe it.**

Modern Parallels

Think of how people today flock to **online conspiracy theories**—claims that a celebrity has secretly returned from the dead, or that a mysterious prophet has "the real answers."

Jesus is saying:

"Don't get caught in the noise. Don't chase shadows."

We live in an age of **viral lies**:

- YouTube "prophets"

- Instagram "apostles"

- TikTok preachers
  All claiming to have received secret revelations from God.

Over the years, **thousands have been deceived** by people claiming to be the **reincarnation of Jesus Christ**.

But Jesus is saying:

"When I return, **you'll know**. There will be **no need to guess**."

And let's talk frankly:

There are **thousands of keyboard warriors** online today, all claiming they know who the Antichrist is.

But hear this—

When a charming, charismatic man rises on the world stage...

And he brokers a seven-year peace treaty in the Middle East...
And that deal is signed, sealed, and set in motion...

Then—and only then—will you know who the Antichrist is.

Until then:
Stay grounded.
Stay wise.
Stay in the Word.

Because **truth** is not trending—it's eternal.

"For as lightning that comes from the east is visible even in the west, so will be the coming of the Son of Man." – *Matthew 24:27*

Jesus is making something abundantly clear here:
His return will be visible, global, and impossible to ignore.
Like a sudden flash of lightning that streaks across the sky and lights up the whole horizon—
His coming will not be private or hidden.

Picture This:

Think of a violent thunderstorm rolling across the skies of London.
You don't need someone to nudge you and say, "Hey, look!"
The windows rattle. The clouds explode with light. Thunder roars.
It grabs your attention whether you're indoors or outside—**you can't miss it**.

In the same way, **when Jesus returns, it will shake the heavens**.
It won't be announced quietly. It won't be confined to a location.
The entire world will witness the King of Kings break through the clouds in power and glory.

Let This Sink In:

There will be **no guesswork**, no need for spiritual speculation.
You won't have to rely on prophets, blogs, or viral videos.
You won't need someone to say, "He's in the desert!" or "He's in this secret room!"

When Jesus returns, **every screen, every soul, every nation will know.**
No one will miss it. No one will mistake it.

So What Should We Do?

- You don't need to live in fear that you'll miss it.

- You don't need to obsess over every strange headline or conspiracy theory.

- You don't need to chase every so-called prophet who claims "special revelation."

Instead—**get ready by being grounded.**
Let your heart burn for Christ, not for clues.
Let your life be a testimony, not a treasure map.
Let your hands be busy serving, not speculating.

Be Ready. Stay Ready.

Keep your heart ready—not your binoculars.
Be watchful, be faithful, and be found doing what He's called you to do.

Because when He comes... He comes in glory.
Not as a whisper, but as a roar.
Not in secret, but for the world to see.
And every eye will witness the return of the rightful King.

"Wherever there is a carcass, there the vultures will gather." – Matthew 24:28

At first glance, this may sound cryptic—but Jesus is using a vivid, natural image to make a profound spiritual point.
Dead things attract vultures. It's a law of nature. But Jesus is saying more than that.

A Deeper Meaning

Where there is **spiritual death**, deception, judgement, and destruction follow.
When people reject truth—when a society turns from God—they become easy prey.
Falsehood feeds on what's already dying.

Think of a culture where morality collapses. Greed, violence, hatred, perversion—**this is the carcass.**

And just like in nature, **the vultures come:** False teaching, spiritual blindness, political chaos, broken families, and division.

Today's World

Look around:
War zones.
Political corruption.
Children trafficked and exploited.
Truth replaced with "my truth."
A world **rotting without God.**

It's not just decay—it's spiritual death. And where there is death, the vultures are circling.

But Here's the Hope

Jesus wasn't just pointing out the decay— He was **warning us to recognise the signs** before the final judgement.

Where darkness reigns, vultures gather.
But where **Christ returns**, light breaks through the darkness.

The world may be rotting in places, but the story doesn't end there.
Jesus is coming—and with Him, justice, healing, and resurrection.

Chapter 8

The Sky Will Shake, But the Word Will Stand

"Immediately after the distress of those days, 'the sun will be darkened, and the moon will not give its light; the stars will fall from the sky, and the heavenly bodies will be shaken.'" – Matthew 24:29

This verse carries both **literal and symbolic** significance.

On one level, Jesus is describing a **cosmic disturbance**—a real, physical upheaval in the natural world.

Events like the darkening of the sun and moon, the falling of stars, and the trembling of the heavens are used throughout Scripture as signs of **divine judgement** and the **breaking in of God's Kingdom**.

But it goes deeper than that. It's also **profoundly symbolic**.

The Shaking of What Seems Unshakable

The sun, moon, and stars are things we regard as fixed and permanent—forces beyond human control.

Jesus is saying that **even the most enduring elements of creation will be shaken**.

It's a striking image: the **unravelling of everything humanity places its trust in**—security, stability, permanence.

Imagine This...

Picture your life as a structure built on foundations you rely on:

- Government

- The economy

- Your health

- The climate

- Your relationships

Now imagine all those supports **trembling at once**.

The sun goes dark—no more clarity.
The moon gives no light—no guidance in the

night.
The stars fall—those distant anchors by which sailors once navigated, suddenly gone.

What happens when **everything you thought was stable begins to collapse**?

This Is More Than Ancient Prophecy

It's a **deeply personal question**:
What are you clinging to when the world begins to fall apart?

This moment in Scripture challenges us to **examine where we place our trust**.
Are we rooted in what is eternal, or tied to things that can be shaken?

Here Is the Hope

Even if the sky falls and the stars vanish, **God's Word remains unshaken**.

He is not surprised by crisis, chaos, or collapse.
He told us **in advance**—not to frighten us, but to **prepare us**.

When Jesus describes these signs, it's not to overwhelm us.
It's an **invitation into deeper trust**.

This passage is not only about judgement—it's about **readiness**.
It reminds us that what we see with our eyes is **not the whole story**.
God's purposes are still unfolding, even when the world seems to be unravelling.

A Final Truth

When your life is anchored in Christ, you are **not shaken by the shaking**.
You are held steady by something stronger than the sun, the moon, or the stars—
you are held by the One who made them.

"Then will appear the sign of the Son of Man in heaven. And then all the peoples of the earth will mourn when they see the Son of Man coming on the clouds of heaven, with power and great glory." – Matthew 24:30

This is the **return of Jesus**—**glorious, powerful**, and **visible to all**.
Some will mourn because they **rejected Him**.
But for **believers**, this is our **blessed hope**.

The King Returns

When a king comes to reclaim his throne, **everyone takes notice**.
The traitors **tremble**—but the faithful **rejoice**.

We do not need to look to elections, governments, or parliaments for our salvation.
One day, Jesus will return—**not as a baby in a manger**, but as the **King of Kings** and **Lord of Lords**.

Let the World Laugh... for Now

Let the world laugh.
Let them mock.
Let them dismiss the truth.

But when He returns, **every eye will see**.
Every tongue will confess—
"Jesus is Lord."

"And he will send his angels with a loud trumpet call, and they will gather his elect from the four winds, from one end of the heavens to the other." — Matthew 24:31

Jesus is not returning to bring fear, but to **gather His people**.
This is not a message of panic, but of **promise**.

You are **not forgotten**.
No matter where life has scattered you, God knows exactly where you are.
When the time comes, He will send His angels to bring you **home**.

Picture a mother standing at the edge of a playground at dusk, calling for her children to come in.
Some are nearby, others have wandered far—but she knows each one by name.
She will not leave until every child is safely gathered in.

In the same way, when the trumpet sounds, Jesus will send His angels across the earth—not one of His people will be overlooked.
Not one will be left behind.

Encouragement:

Some of you feel **lost** in this world.
You may feel invisible—buried under grief, regret, loneliness, or shame.
But **heaven has not lost track of you**.

God knows your **name**, your **story**, your **pain**, and your **position**—spiritually and literally.
He knows exactly where you are, and exactly how to reach you.

You may feel scattered, but you are never **abandoned**.
You may feel small, but you are **child of God**.

When that trumpet call echoes across the heavens, it will not be a sound of fear for the believer.
It will be the call to **come home**.
The final gathering.
The great reunion.
The moment when all that has been broken is restored, and every distance is closed.

Conclusion:

Jesus is coming back—not as a stranger, but as a **Saviour**.
Not with judgement for His elect, but with **joy**.

Let this truth settle deep in your soul:
You are not forgotten. You are not forsaken. You are not alone.
The angels are coming for you.
And when that trumpet sounds, it will be the sweetest sound you've ever heard.
A call not to run or hide, but to rise—and **go home**.

"Now learn this lesson from the fig tree: As soon as its twigs get tender and its leaves come out, you know that summer is near. Even so, when you see all these things, you know that it is near, right at the door."
— Matthew 24:32–33

Jesus is teaching His followers to be **spiritually discerning**.
Just as we can tell summer is approaching when the trees begin to bud, we must learn to recognise the spiritual signs that point to His return.

In Britain, we don't look at fig trees—we look for **daffodils**.

When they bloom, we know spring has arrived.

Likewise, Jesus says that when we see global unrest and moral upheaval, we shouldn't respond with fear, but with **faith**.

These are not just random events—they are reminders: **He is near.**

Today's Signs

Earthquakes.
Wars and rumours of war.
Pandemics.
Widespread deception.
Hatred growing cold.
Persecution of believers.
The gospel being preached in every nation.

These are not the end—but they are the **birth pains**.

Hope at the Door

When a mother goes into labour, the pain signals that **new life is on the way**.

In the same way, the shaking of this world points to the **soon return of Jesus**.

Don't be disheartened by what's going wrong around you.
Be encouraged by what it means:
Your King is at the door.

Reflection

What are the "fig tree signs" in your life today?
Are you noticing the spiritual season changing around you?

Take a moment to pause and reflect—not on the chaos of the world, but on the constancy of Christ. He said He would return—and every shaking is a reminder, not of fear, but of hope.

Ask yourself:
Am I living with expectation, or distraction?
Am I watching the signs with faith, or with worry?

Let this be a gentle wake-up call.
Not to panic—but to prepare.
Not to hide—but to hope.

Because your Saviour isn't far off.
He's at the door.

"Truly I tell you, this generation will certainly not pass away until all these things have happened." — Matthew 24:34

There has long been debate over what Jesus meant by **"this generation."**
Was He referring to the generation alive at that time?
Or the generation that witnesses the signs of the end?
Some believe it refers to the Jewish people, who will endure until all is fulfilled.

Whatever the interpretation, **Jesus' message is clear**:
There is urgency. The clock is ticking.

You're not watching a rehearsal.
This is the final act.

Live like the curtain could fall at any moment.

Challenge

Don't waste your life waiting for a perfect moment.
Serve with passion. Love without hesitation. Preach boldly. Forgive freely.

Time is short—and eternity is long.

Reflection

Jesus reminds us that time is moving quickly toward fulfilment. Whether "this generation" refers to a specific group or era, the message is clear: don't live as if tomorrow is guaranteed. The signs are unfolding, and the moment of His return is closer than ever. Each day is an opportunity—to love more deeply, speak truth more boldly, and walk in faith more fully. You're not on standby. You're on assignment.

Question

If you truly believed Jesus could return in your lifetime, how would it change the way you live today?

"Heaven and earth will pass away, but my words will never pass away." — Matthew 24:35

Everything we see and experience—**nations, wealth, fame, technology, even the heavens above**—will eventually fade.

The things we so often chase, protect, and prioritise are temporary.

But Jesus draws a powerful contrast:
His Word will never pass away.
It will **outlast the stars**, **outlive the earth**, and **remain unchanged** when everything else collapses.

A World That's Always Changing

Empires rise and fall.
Kings and queens are crowned—and buried.
Technology becomes outdated in months.
Today's cultural truths are tomorrow's forgotten trends.

Even the strongest human achievements cannot withstand time.
But the Word of God endures.

Open your Bible today and what do you find?
The same message that sustained the early church.
The same hope that has comforted martyrs, missionaries, prisoners, and seekers for centuries.
Still alive. Still speaking. Still powerful.

Today's World

In our culture, people build their lives on what is popular:

- Trends

- Science

- Public opinion

- Political ideologies

But none of these things have the power to **redeem your soul** or **carry you through eternity**.
When the world shifts and shakes, only one foundation remains: **God's Word**.

Let His Word Be:

- Your **anchor** in the storm, when life feels chaotic

- Your **compass** in the fog, when direction is unclear

- Your **fire** in the night, when hope feels distant

Let Scripture be more than words on a page—
Let it be **the voice that steadies your heart**, the **truth that shapes your mind**, and the **lamp that lights your path**.

Reflection

Everything around us is shifting. The world we once knew is changing faster than ever—values, systems, beliefs, even what's considered truth.
But in the midst of uncertainty, **God's Word remains fixed**.

Take a moment to ask yourself:
What am I building my life upon?
Is it something that will pass away—or something eternal?

God's Word is not just a historical document.
It is **alive**, **relevant**, and **unchanging**.
When everything else fades, His promises remain.

Let it quiet your fears.
Let it re-centre your perspective.

Let it remind you that **you are standing on something eternal**.

"Christian, you are not waiting for the world to be fixed.

You are waiting for the King to return.

Let your lamp burn bright, for the Bridegroom is coming."

Chapter 9

The Groom Is Coming

"But about that day or hour no one knows, not even the angels in heaven, nor the Son, but only the Father." — Matthew 24:34

Jesus makes it absolutely clear—**no one knows the exact moment of His return.** Not the angels. Not even Himself at that time. **Only the Father knows.**

But this wasn't just a mystery statement; it was a **deeply familiar image** to Jesus' first-century Galilean audience.

The Betrothal (A Covenant Promise)

In Galilean Jewish culture, **weddings followed a unique and powerful pattern—**

and Jesus often used this to explain spiritual truths.

A young couple would begin with **a betrothal**—a legally binding covenant similar to marriage, although they wouldn't live together yet.

At this point, the **bridegroom would leave** to prepare a place for his bride, typically building an extension onto his father's house.

This is exactly the language Jesus used in **John 14:2–3**:

"In my Father's house are many rooms... I go to prepare a place for you... and I will come again and take you to myself."

Preparation—and the Secrecy of the Timing

During this preparation time, **only the father of the groom** could decide when the new home was complete and everything was ready.
The **son couldn't fetch his bride until the father gave permission**.

So when Jesus says,

"No one knows the day or the hour... only the Father,"
He's speaking in familiar wedding terms—His audience would have instantly understood the **imagery of anticipation and honour**.

The Shofar and the Surprise Arrival

Once the father gave the word—**"Son, go get your bride!"**—
the bridegroom would gather his friends, and with great excitement, **blow the shofar** (ram's horn) to announce his coming.

The bride would typically be **watching and waiting**, not knowing the exact hour—
but her **lamp was lit**, her **garments were ready**, and her **heart was prepared**.

This tradition is beautifully mirrored in **Matthew 25**, the parable of the ten virgins—some were ready, some were not.

The Wedding and Celebration

The bridegroom often arrived **at night** with a **shout** and the **sound of the shofar**.

This is a direct parallel with **1 Thessalonians 4:16**:

"For the Lord Himself will come down from heaven, with a loud command, with the voice of the archangel and with the trumpet call of God..."

The bride was **lifted up**, often carried in a bridal litter to the father's house—
a stunning picture of believers being **caught up to meet Christ in the air**.

"Then we who are alive and remain shall be caught up together... to meet the Lord in the air."
— *1 Thessalonians 4:17*

Spiritual Insight for Today

Jesus wasn't just speaking in metaphor—He was painting **a prophetic picture**.
The Church is His bride.
He has made a **covenant** with us.
He has gone to **prepare a place** for us.

And **He will return suddenly**, at a time only the Father knows.

Those who are watching and ready will **join the wedding celebration**.

Connection to the Rapture and the Marriage Supper

In Galilean weddings, once the groom came and took his bride, the doors to the feast were **shut**. Even invited guests who came late were **not allowed in**.

Being on the guest list wasn't enough—you had to be **ready**.

This reflects Jesus' warning: **many have heard the invitation**, but only the ready will enter in.
It also beautifully aligns with the view of the **pre-tribulation rapture**, and the **Marriage Supper of the Lamb** in Revelation 19.

Illustration:

It's like waiting for a surprise inspection at work.

If the boss says, *"I'll come sometime this week,"*
You don't wait until the last minute—you **stay ready every day**.
You tidy your desk, prepare your reports, and watch the door.

Why?
Because you **don't know** when he's coming—but you **know** he is.

Or what about this scenario:

Imagine your house is a mess—clothes everywhere, dishes piled high, takeaway boxes on the table.
Then your phone rings:
"Hey! Just letting you know—I'm five minutes away!"
It's your mum. Or your pastor. Or worse... your in-laws.

Panic mode.
You're sprinting through the house like an Olympic cleaner—throwing socks under the sofa, stuffing dishes in the oven, and lighting a candle like it will fix everything.

Why?
Because someone important is coming—and **you weren't ready**.

Now imagine if Jesus gave you that call.
Except... He won't.
There won't be a five-minute warning.

That's why He told us: **stay ready**.
Don't wait to scramble your faith together when the sky splits open.

Live ready.
Don't tidy your spiritual house in a panic— keep it clean every day.

Today's World:

People today pour energy into trying to **predict** the end—through charts, dates, codes, and theories.
But Jesus said even He didn't know the hour—**so why should we pretend we do?**

The focus is not on prediction.
It's on **preparation**.

Reflection

Jesus isn't asking us to figure out when He'll return—He's asking us to be ready.

Like the Galilean bride waiting in joyful expectation, we're not meant to live in fear, but in **faithful anticipation**.
He has gone to prepare a place for us.
He has promised to return.
And when He comes, it won't be with whispers—it will be with a shout, a trumpet blast, and glory that shakes the heavens.

But the question is not *when* He'll return.
It's whether **you'll be ready** when He does.

Are your spiritual garments clean?
Is your lamp burning?
Are you watching the signs or sleeping through them?

This isn't about paranoia. It's about preparation.
It's about living each day as though the sky could open tonight.
Because one day—it will.

Chapter 10

As It Was In the Days of Noah - Part One

When Jesus spoke of the end times, He didn't reference world powers or political systems first—He pointed to the days of Noah. Why? Because the heart of humanity in Noah's time mirrors our world today: a society drowning in sin, mocking righteousness, and blind to what's coming. Jesus wasn't being poetic—He was issuing a prophetic warning.

"As it was in the days of Noah, so it will be at the coming of the Son of Man. For in the days before the flood, people were eating and drinking, marrying and giving in marriage, up to the day Noah entered the ark; and they knew nothing about what would happen until the flood came and took them all away. That is how it will be at the coming of the Son of Man."— Matthew 24:36-39

That's a powerful and sobering statement. Jesus wasn't simply offering a metaphor—He was issuing a warning. As we look at the world around us, it's clear: we are again living in days of spiritual rebellion, moral decline, and even scientific tampering with the very fabric of God's creation.

A. Moral and Spiritual Rebellion
Just like back then:

- Violence fills the earth

- Perversion is celebrated

- Truth is mocked

- The fear of God is absent

- Wickedness is mainstream

2 Timothy 3:1–4 says: "But mark this: There will be terrible times in the last days. People will be lovers of themselves, lovers of money, boastful, proud, abusive, disobedient to their parents, ungrateful, unholy, without love, unforgiving, slanderous, without self-control, brutal, not lovers of the good, treacherous, rash, conceited, lovers of pleasure rather than lovers of God."

Sound familiar? The spirit of the age mirrors the spirit of Noah's time. When Jesus said, "As it was in the days of Noah, so it will be at the coming of the Son of Man," He wasn't just using poetic language—He was pointing to a time marked by rampant corruption and godlessness as a signpost for us today.

1. Corruption of Creation

Genesis 6:1–5 tells us: "When human beings began to increase in number on the earth and daughters were born to them, the sons of God saw that the daughters of humans were beautiful, and they married any of them they chose... The Nephilim were on the earth in those days... They were the heroes of old, men of renown. The Lord saw how great the wickedness of the human race had become..."

In those ancient days, the world wasn't just sinful—it was corrupted at a foundational level. The "sons of God," widely understood as fallen angels, crossed a divine boundary by taking human wives. The result? The Nephilim—giant, hybrid beings that distorted the human genetic line.

This wasn't ordinary sin—it was a direct violation of God's created order. Humanity was being tampered with. These beings were unnatural, violent, and unredeemable—the fruit of spiritual rebellion at a genetic level.

Jude 1:6–7 backs this up: "And the angels who did not keep their proper domain, but left their own abode, He has reserved in everlasting chains under darkness for the judgment of the great day..."

Genesis 6:12 further clarifies: "God saw how corrupt the earth had become, for all the people on earth had corrupted their ways."

This is why God sent the flood—not out of cruelty, but to protect the future bloodline through which the Messiah would come.

Genesis 6:9 says: "Noah was a righteous man, blameless among the people of his time, and he walked faithfully with God."

That word "blameless" (Hebrew: tamim) can also be understood to mean untainted—his lineage was uncorrupted, preserving what God had originally designed.

2. History Is Repeating Itself

Jesus said the days before His return would mirror those of Noah. Let's examine our own time:

DNA Alteration and Gene Editing

In our generation, we are witnessing a technological revolution in genetics that would have sounded like science fiction just decades ago. At the forefront is a tool called **CRISPR** (Clustered Regularly Interspaced Short Palindromic Repeats) — a groundbreaking gene-editing technology that allows scientists to "cut and paste" sections of DNA with precision.

While the original intent of CRISPR was to eliminate genetic disorders and fight disease — which is a noble goal — the door has now been opened to far more controversial applications.

Let's look at some of the developments already happening:

Designer Babies

Scientists are now able to manipulate embryos to select preferred traits before birth — such as eye colour, height, intelligence, and resistance to disease.

This is not hypothetical. In 2018, a Chinese scientist announced the birth of the world's first gene-edited babies, sparking global outrage and concern. The children's DNA was edited to make them immune to HIV. But the long-term effects are unknown.

What begins as the desire to "improve" humanity soon becomes a step towards eugenics — deciding which lives are more desirable than others.

Synthetic Embryos Without Sperm or Egg

Researchers have now created embryo-like structures from stem cells without using traditional reproductive methods. These "embryos" contain the beginnings of organs — a beating heart, a brain, and even early nervous systems.

They are not technically human — and yet they mimic early human life. This raises enormous ethical questions:

What are we creating?
Where is the line between life and experiment?

Human-Animal Hybrids (Chimeras)

Scientists are also experimenting with **chimeras** — mixing human and animal cells to grow organs for transplant. Human cells have been placed in pig and monkey embryos in the hope of growing replacement hearts, livers, and kidneys.

While this may sound compassionate in theory, it enters dangerously murky territory. We are blurring the boundaries of species — merging God's distinct creations.

This is no longer healing the sick — it's rewriting the script of life itself.

These are not far-future predictions — they are **today's headlines**.

We are altering the very **blueprint of life** — the DNA that God wrote into every cell.

Just like in the days of Noah, there is a **corruption of creation** taking place.

Back then, fallen angels tampered with humanity at a genetic level, producing hybrid beings unrecognisable from God's original design.

Now, with the rise of gene-editing tools, synthetic embryos, and chimeric experiments, we are once again **tampering with what it means to be human**.

The warning signs are clear.
We are walking in the shadow of Genesis 6.

In Noah's day, corruption came from fallen angels tampering with humanity. Today, it comes from laboratories, biotech firms, and AI-driven dreams of immortality. What once happened through supernatural rebellion is now happening through scientific pride. And the results may be even more dangerous.

As It Was In the Days of Noah

Part Two

Tampering with the Image of God

Humanity has once again reached for the divine — not by prayer or worship, but by rewriting the very code of life. We are no longer satisfied with being created in God's image. We want to improve it, edit it, upgrade it. But in our quest to become more, are we becoming something less?

mRNA Technologies and Genetic Reprogramming

The emergence of **mRNA technology** marked a revolutionary moment in modern science and medicine. Most notably introduced to the public through the development of COVID-19 vaccines, mRNA platforms have taken us into uncharted biological territory — not merely treating illness, but actively instructing the body to behave in new ways.

Let's break it down:

What is mRNA?

Messenger RNA (mRNA) is a molecule that delivers coded instructions to your cells, telling them what proteins to make. Traditionally, your body does this naturally as part of everyday function — DNA in your cell nucleus gives the orders, and mRNA carries them out.

However, mRNA vaccines work **by bypassing your DNA** and delivering **external genetic instructions** directly into your cells. Instead of using a piece of the virus (as with traditional vaccines), they tell your cells **to manufacture a synthetic version of the virus's spike protein**, which your immune system then recognises and responds to.

This is more than a jab — it's reprogramming.

For the first time in history, we are using technology to **rewrite our biology** on the go.

This isn't just treating symptoms or even curing disease — it's **bioengineering at a molecular level**.

Now, let's be clear:

mRNA vaccines were presented as a powerful tool in responding to the pandemic, and many see them as a scientific success. But we must not ignore the broader implications.

A New Era of Medicine — and of Risk
This technology opens doors to countless future applications:

- mRNA treatments for cancer

- Customisable immune responses

- Gene therapies to prevent inherited conditions

But what happens when this power is misused? What safeguards are in place to prevent permanent damage to our genetic makeup?
How do we evaluate the long-term effects when the science itself is only a few years old?

We must ask: **What is the cost of speed?**
Have we moved so fast in pursuit of control over illness that we've overstepped our bounds as created beings?

A Theological Concern

As believers, we are not called to reject medicine or science. But we are called to discern the times.

God designed the human body with astonishing complexity and wisdom. When we begin rewriting His code, we must do so with fear, reverence, and humility — or not at all.

Just as in the days of Noah, humanity is once again **tampering with the sacred**.
Not through fallen angels this time, but through laboratories, peer-reviewed journals, and billion-pound biotech companies.

We are no longer simply **treating life** — we are **redefining it**.

And Scripture warns:

"Professing themselves to be wise, they became fools..." (Romans 1:22)

Transhumanism: The New Tower of Babel

The word *Transhumanism* might sound like science fiction — something from a dystopian novel or Hollywood blockbuster — but it is no longer a futuristic fantasy. It is **today's reality**, and it's advancing at astonishing speed.

At its core, transhumanism is the belief that humanity can and should **evolve beyond its natural state** by merging with advanced technology — enhancing the body, upgrading the brain, and ultimately redefining what it means to be human.

This is not just about health or healing. This is about **transcending humanity**.

What Does This Look Like Today?

Transhumanist technologies are no longer theoretical. They're being actively developed, tested, and funded by the world's most powerful governments, militaries, and tech giants:

- **Neural implants**, such as *Neuralink*, are designed to connect the brain directly to the internet, enabling people to control devices with thought, store memories externally, and interface with artificial intelligence.

- **AI-human integration**, where advanced algorithms are paired with human biology to augment decision-making, memory recall, and even emotional regulation.

- **Bionic limbs and artificial organs**, offering superhuman strength, speed, and endurance — not merely restoring what was lost, but exceeding natural design.

- **Genetic enhancement**, using CRISPR and related tools to edit DNA before birth — not only to cure disease, but to select traits such as height, intelligence, and even temperament.

- **Human-animal chimeras**, where animal DNA is being spliced with human genes for experimental growth of organs and tissue — a line dangerously reminiscent of the hybrid beings of Genesis 6.

- **Biometric surveillance**, with facial recognition, gait analysis, and even **brainwave tracking**, already operational in nations like China, and rapidly expanding elsewhere.

DARPA and the Rise of "Super Soldiers"

Perhaps the most chilling development comes from the military sector. Agencies like **DARPA** (Defence Advanced Research Projects Agency) — a branch of the U.S. Department of Defence — are developing **genetically and cybernetically enhanced soldiers.**

These experimental "super soldiers" are being engineered to:

- **Require little to no sleep**

- **Feel significantly less pain**

- **Process and react faster than average humans**

- **Communicate telepathically via brain-to-brain interfaces**

- **Possess augmented reality displays inside their vision**

This is no longer the realm of comic books — it is being designed, tested, and funded with billions of dollars.

The goal is to **create the ultimate human weapon** — one that surpasses ordinary human limitations and is tied, not just biologically, but digitally, to its command structure.

A New Tower of Babel

Make no mistake — this is **not just technological evolution**. This is **spiritual rebellion** dressed in silicone and code.

It echoes the arrogance of Genesis 11, where humanity declared:

"Come, let us build ourselves a city, with a tower that reaches to the heavens, so that we may make a name for ourselves..."
(Genesis 11:4)

Back then, they sought heaven by stacking bricks. Today, we seek it through bytes, implants, and genetically reprogrammed cells. Once again, we are declaring: *"We can be like gods."*

The Ancient Lie, Upgraded

This is the same serpent's lie repackaged for the modern world:

"You will not surely die... For God knows that when you eat of it your eyes will be opened, and you will be like God..."
(Genesis 3:4–5)

This lie has simply evolved. Instead of a forbidden fruit, we now have a microchip. Instead of a serpent, we have scientific institutions. Instead of Eden, we have the lab and the launchpad.

And just like in Genesis 6, the image of God in mankind is under attack — not by Nephilim, but by our own hands.

The Theological Cost

What does it mean to be made in God's image — if that image is overwritten by artificial intelligence?

What does it mean to be human — if our minds are altered, our bodies genetically restructured, and our dependence on the Creator replaced by machines?

Transhumanism undermines:

- **The sanctity of the body**

- **The necessity of the soul**

- **The sufficiency of God's design**

By tampering with God's blueprint, we're not progressing — we're **regressing into rebellion**.

The world is building a new Tower of Babel, this time with microchips instead of bricks. But just like before, judgment will come. The question is — will you be caught inside the tower, or inside the Ark?

As It Was In the Days of Noah

Part Three

Before the Door Shuts

The flood didn't fall without warning. For over a century, God extended mercy through Noah — a preacher, a builder, a prophet. And yet, only eight people entered the ark. Not because space ran out, but because belief never started. Today, we live in the final minutes before another door closes.

Where Does This Lead?

The path of transhumanism leads to **dehumanisation**, **spiritual deception**, and ultimately judgment.

It offers a false salvation: *"We will defeat death. We will evolve. We will be eternal."*
But there is **only one resurrection**, and it does not come through code or science — it comes through Christ.

We are once again in the days of Noah — a time of hybridisation, rebellion, and deep corruption. But just as God provided an ark back then, He has provided one now:

Jesus is the Ark. The Cross is the Door. The Time is Now.

3. Noah Warned Them – But They Ignored Him

Imagine this: God tells a man to build a gigantic boat — not near the sea, but in the middle of dry land — and not just a little dinghy, but a floating zoo. Oh, and one more thing — it had **never rained** before.

Yes, you read that correctly. According to Genesis 2:5–6, rain wasn't part of the earth's early climate system:

"For the Lord God had not sent rain on the earth... but streams came up from the earth and watered the whole surface of the ground."
(Genesis 2:5–6)

Back then, the earth was watered by a mist or underground springs — so the idea of water falling from the sky must have sounded like something out of a fantasy story.

So picture Noah hammering away for 100 years, building this massive vessel in his back garden while neighbours strolled by with their morning coffee, shaking their heads:

"Alright Noah, still building that boat in the middle of nowhere? You do know we don't get floods around here, right?"

"What's this 'rain' you keep talking about? Never seen it, mate."

"You've been at this for decades! You sure you're not just avoiding chores?"

They mocked him relentlessly. **For over a century**, Noah warned them about coming judgment — not just with his words, but with his obedience. His ark was a sermon in wood and pitch. But no one listened.

Jesus captured this moment perfectly in Matthew 24:39:

"They knew nothing about what would happen until the flood came and took them all away."

They were warned — repeatedly. They had time. But they refused to take it seriously.

Mockery, Delay... and Then the Rain Came

People today are no different.

"You Christians have been saying Jesus is coming back for 2,000 years!"

"I'll believe it when I see it."

"Why worry? The world's always had problems."

It's the same spirit of apathy, the same mocking tone. Just like in Noah's time, people today live with their eyes on the immediate — eating, drinking, marrying, holiday planning, Instagramming — as if history is on pause and judgment is just a fairy tale.

But when the rain came in Noah's day — it came **suddenly**.

"The Lord shut him in."
(Genesis 7:16)

Once the door of the ark was closed, it was **sealed by God** — not even Noah could open it. Then, for the first time in history, the skies burst open.

Can you imagine the panic?

Neighbours who had laughed came running, banging on the ark:

"Noah! You were right! Let us in!"
"We believe you now! Just open the door!"

But it was too late. The time for mercy had passed. The door of salvation had shut.

A Modern Parallel

Imagine a family ignoring wildfire evacuation orders. Instead, they decide to have a barbecue.

They say:

"We've heard these warnings before. They always blow over."

But this time, the fire is real. By the time the smoke thickens and flames are visible, it's too late to escape.

That's the picture Jesus paints for us. That's the urgency.

Today's World – Distracted and Asleep

Let's be honest: we're too busy for eternity. Distracted by TikTok, sedated by Netflix, and scrolling our way through the apocalypse.

Jesus said in Luke 17:26–27:

"Just as it was in the days of Noah, so also will it be in the days of the Son of Man. People were eating, drinking, marrying and being given in marriage up to the day Noah entered the ark. Then the flood came and destroyed them all."

Life was moving on — weddings, business deals, gym memberships. Everything seemed "normal." Then judgment fell.

Not because people were particularly evil in their day-to-day lives — but because they were **spiritually asleep**, indifferent to God, and deaf to His warnings.

A Serious Reminder

Here's the truth: God didn't send the flood without warning.

He gave 120 years of mercy (Genesis 6:3). He raised up a preacher (2 Peter 2:5 calls Noah "a preacher of righteousness"). He made the ark big enough to save many — but only eight entered.

The issue wasn't that God wasn't clear.
The issue was that people didn't care.

And we are once again living in that time.

The ark today isn't made of gopher wood — it's made of grace. It's the cross. And the door is still open.

But it won't stay open forever.

4. The Gospel — Our Ark Today

In Noah's time, **the ark was the only means of escape** from the judgment that was about to fall upon a corrupt and violent world. It wasn't just a boat—it was **a vessel of mercy**, handcrafted by God's instruction and built in faith by Noah. All who entered it were saved. All who remained outside were lost.

Today, we are not looking to a wooden ark for salvation. **Our Ark is the Cross.**
And just like in Noah's time, **there is only one way to be saved**.

A Shadow of Things to Come

The Apostle Peter makes a striking comparison:

"...God waited patiently in the days of Noah while the ark was being built. In it only a few people, eight in all, were saved through water, and this water symbolises baptism that now saves you also—not the removal of dirt from the body but the pledge of a clear conscience toward God.
It saves you by the resurrection of Jesus Christ."
— 1 Peter 3:20–21

Peter isn't saying we are saved by ritual. He's saying that just as **the ark bore Noah and his family safely above the waters of judgment**, so now **Jesus carries us through** the waters of God's righteous wrath—not by wood and pitch, but by blood and grace.

The ark was a foreshadowing—a type. The Cross is the fulfilment.

Jesus Took the Flood for Us

At the Cross, Jesus endured **the full downpour of God's judgment**—not for His own sin (He had none), but for ours. He became the substitute, the sacrifice, the shelter.

He stood in our place, taking the flood so we wouldn't drown.

"Surely he took up our pain and bore our suffering...
But he was pierced for our transgressions,
he was crushed for our iniquities...
and by his wounds we are healed."
— Isaiah 53:4–5

Where the ark was made of gopher wood and sealed with pitch, **our salvation was sealed with blood**—the blood of the spotless Lamb of God.

The Way Into the Ark

Salvation is not earned. It is not inherited. It is not awarded for good behaviour.

It is received by faith in Christ—**the only doorway into safety**.

"If you declare with your mouth, 'Jesus is Lord,' and believe in your heart that God raised Him from the dead,
you will be saved."
— Romans 10:9

This is the Gospel:
Jesus lived the life we could not live.
He died the death we deserved to die.
He rose so we could rise with Him.

Just as Noah entered the ark through one door, we enter into life **through Christ**, who said:

"I am the door; if anyone enters through Me, he will be saved."
— John 10:9

5. Final Call — Get in the Ark

In Noah's time, when the ark was finally complete and the animals had entered, something significant happened—**God Himself shut the door** (Genesis 7:16). The moment that door closed, the time of mercy ended, and the time of judgement began. No one else could enter. It was final.

Jesus told us that just like in Noah's day, His return will catch people off guard. Life will feel normal—meals, weddings, holidays, shopping, work—until suddenly, everything changes.

"But they knew nothing about what would happen until the flood came and took them all away. That is how it will be at the coming of the Son of Man."
— Matthew 24:39

People had years to listen to Noah's warnings. But they ignored him—just like many today ignore the call of the Gospel.

If You Don't Know Jesus

Let's be honest—life moves fast. We're busy. We get distracted. Maybe you've heard it all before:

- "I'll sort my life out first."

- "I'm not ready."

- "Maybe when I'm older."

- "Is this even real?"

But what if the door closed today?

"I tell you, now is the time of God's favour, now is the day of salvation."
— *2 Corinthians 6:2*

You don't need to fix yourself before coming to God. You just need to **come**. Jesus is the Ark—the only safe place in the storm to come. And the door is still open.

All He asks is that you put your trust in Him.

"If you declare with your mouth, 'Jesus is Lord,' and believe in your heart that God raised him from the dead, you will be saved."
— *Romans 10:9*

If You Already Believe

Then it's time to **live like you do**:

- Speak up when others stay silent.

- Live clean when others chase compromise.

- Share truth when others spread lies.

- Keep your lamp burning when the world falls asleep.

Noah wasn't just saved for himself—he was chosen to **preserve life**, to build something that would rescue others. So are you.

"By faith Noah... in holy fear built an ark to save his family."
— Hebrews 11:7

You're not here to fit in—you're here to **stand out**.

Imagine the news reports say there's a tsunami coming. You live near the coast. Emergency services issue warnings, but most people carry on like normal. They've heard it before.

One neighbour listens. He packs up his family and drives inland.

The others stay. "It's just hype," they say.

Then one morning the sea suddenly pulls back—and before anyone can react, the wave hits. The window for escape is gone.

That's what Jesus meant. His return will come quickly. The time to prepare is **now**.

Final Thoughts

Jesus is coming.
The days of Noah are here.
And the Ark is ready.

Don't get caught outside the door.

Reflection Question

If the flood came tomorrow, would you be inside the Ark? Or would you be banging on the door too late?

The Ark is ready. The Cross is the door. You are invited in. But soon — very soon — that door will close. Don't wait.

Chapter 11

Taken or Left — The Rapture and the Ready

"Two men will be in the field; one will be taken and the other left. Two women will be grinding with a hand mill; one will be taken and the other left. Therefore keep watch, because you do not know on what day your Lord will come." — Matthew 24:40-42

This passage lifts the veil on the **sudden and selective** nature of Christ's return. It's not merely a distant prophecy to be studied with detachment — it's a divine interruption that could break into our world **at any moment**.

Jesus is warning us: **be ready**. Not someday. Not eventually. **Now.**

Ordinary Life — Extraordinary Outcome

Notice the setting. These aren't extraordinary scenarios. There's no thunder, no trumpet, no crisis. Just **everyday life**:

- Two men working in a field.

- Two women grinding grain.

They are side by side, in the same environment, doing the same tasks. And yet—**one is taken, the other is left.**

The message? The difference isn't **what** they were doing. It's **who** they belonged to.

This isn't about occupation — it's about orientation.

It's not your job, your church attendance, or your Bible knowledge that qualifies you. It's the **condition of your heart**. It's about whether your life is surrendered to Jesus.

A Matter of the Heart

You can be busy with good things, even "spiritual" things, and still not be ready.

It's possible to be active in ministry but absent in relationship.
To be outwardly engaged, but inwardly distant.
To appear faithful, but be spiritually asleep.

This warning calls us to **live awake** — to cultivate a genuine, ongoing walk with Christ.

Illustration: The Unannounced Visitor

Imagine you're having guests over at some point "this week", but they don't tell you exactly when. You can't risk leaving the house in a mess. You tidy up, not once, but every day — because their arrival is unknown but certain.

In the same way, Jesus tells us not to guess the hour — but to **live in a state of readiness**.

Imagine This:

Two surgeons in the same operating theatre — same qualifications, same years of experience, even the same scalpel in hand.
But only one has properly sterilised instruments.

From the outside, they appear identical.
But one is prepared, the other is not — and lives are at stake.

Or think of two passengers boarding the same flight.
One carries a valid passport and visa. The other does not.

They both board. They both find their seats.
But only one will make it through immigration at the destination.

Today's World: The Illusion of Sameness

In this generation, the illusion of sameness is widespread.

You can be surrounded by believers, serve on a worship team, attend weekly Bible studies, quote verses on social media — and still be spiritually asleep.

Our culture often **confuses closeness to Christian activity with closeness to Christ Himself**.

But Jesus is crystal clear:
Proximity to truth is not the same as preparedness for His return.

He's not calling us to live in anxiety — but in awareness.
Not in panic — but in purpose.
To be **awake, alert, surrendered.**

This Is a Picture of the Rapture

This passage in Matthew foreshadows the coming Rapture —
that divinely appointed moment when Christ will return to gather His people:

"For the Lord himself will come down from heaven, with a loud command,
with the voice of the archangel and with the trumpet call of God,
and the dead in Christ will rise first.
After that, we who are still alive and are left will be caught up together with them in the clouds
to meet the Lord in the air."
— *1 Thessalonians 4:16–17*

It will happen in an instant — no countdown, no alarm, no last-minute delay.
Like lightning flashing across the sky, everything will change in a heartbeat.

People will be going about their lives — working, commuting, shopping, scrolling —
and suddenly, some will vanish.
Taken up to meet the Lord in the air.

Others will be left behind, facing a world spiralling into chaos without the restraining presence of God's people.

It won't matter how **moral**, how **successful**, or how **religiously active** someone appeared to be.
Only those who are **born again**, those who have truly **surrendered to Christ**, will be taken.

There won't be a second chance.
There will be no "pause button" for last-minute decisions.
When it happens — it's final.

"Keep Watch." The Urgency of the Hour

This is not just a warning for the world —
it's a wake-up call for the Church.

Jesus isn't coming with delay.
He's coming with **divine precision**, at **a moment no one expects.**

You won't receive a five-minute warning.
There'll be no time to fumble for your Bible.
No room to try and "get right" at the last second.

The door will be shut or open based on the condition of your heart **right now**.

This moment is **closer than we think**.
The question is not *if* Jesus will return — but *are you ready when He does?*

142

"Therefore, keep watch, because you do not know on what day your Lord will come."
— Matthew 24:42

Reflection: Are You Flight-Ready?

Ask yourself honestly:
If Jesus returned *today*, would you be ready?

Not, "Are you religious enough?"
Not, "Do you attend church?"
But this: **Is your heart surrendered?**

Have you received the gift of salvation through Jesus Christ, or are you relying on your own goodness?

The Rapture won't wait for you to sort things out.
It won't wait for you to be "better" or "almost there."
It will come like a thief in the night — suddenly, unmistakably, finally.

This moment is a mercy. A warning. A window of grace.
Don't put off until tomorrow what eternity demands you settle today.

Illustration: Flight 777 — Ready for Departure

Think of it like this:
We're all aboard **Titus Airlines, Flight 777** — seated, waiting on the runway.

The engines are humming. The cabin lights are dimmed.
You've been handed your ticket — **salvation through Jesus Christ**.

The crew is ready. The destination is prepared.

We're waiting on just one thing: **clearance from Air Traffic Control — God the Father**.

Then suddenly, the announcement will sound:

"Son, go get Your Bride."
You are cleared for takeoff.

In a moment — faster than any jet engine — the flight will lift.
And those who are truly His will be caught up in the clouds to meet the Lord in the air.

The only question is: **Are you on board?**

Chapter 12

The Thief in the Night — Living Like He Could Come Today

"Therefore keep watch, because you do not know on what day your Lord will come.

But understand this: If the owner of the house had known at what time of night the thief was coming,

he would have kept watch and would not have let his house be broken into.

So you also must be ready, because the Son of Man will come at an hour when you do not expect him." — Matthew 24:42-44

Keep Watch: Be Ready, Stay Ready

Jesus doesn't soften the message — He intensifies it.

He doesn't say, *"Relax, it's a long way off,"* or *"You'll get plenty of warning."*
Instead, He speaks with clarity and urgency: **"Be ready."**
His return won't be announced with calendar invites or social media updates.

It won't fit neatly into our schedules or be postponed until we're spiritually sorted.

It will be **sudden** — catching the world off guard.
It will be **deliberate** — part of God's perfect timing, not human expectations.
It will be **divisive** — separating the prepared from the unprepared.

This isn't fear-mongering — it's truth-telling.
Jesus doesn't scare us into obedience. He **loves us into readiness**.

He warns us because He wants us with Him — not left behind.

He compares His return to **a thief in the night**. Not because He's coming to steal or harm, but because a thief never announces his arrival.
He shows up when people are sleeping.
The point is not threat, but **timing**.

A thief doesn't send a countdown. He doesn't knock politely.
He doesn't wait until you're ready. He comes when it's dark, when it's quiet,
when life seems normal — and suddenly, **everything changes**.

That's how Jesus will return.

The day will begin like any other —
Alarm clocks will buzz.
Children will go to school.
People will commute, scroll phones, sip coffee, plan holidays.

And then — in the blink of an eye — **He will come.**

Not to a fanfare of human applause, but to the sound of **a trumpet blast** and **a divine command.**

Not when we're watching the sky — but when most have stopped looking.

This is why Jesus urges us, again and again: **"Be ready. Stay ready. Keep watch."**

Not Passive Watching — Active Readiness

If you knew the exact hour Jesus would return, preparation would be simple.
You'd set a reminder.
You'd clean up your act the night before.
You'd apologise to that person.

Delete the things you shouldn't be watching.
You'd pray with urgency, just in time.

But that's the point — **you don't know the hour**.

No one does.
Not angels. Not prophets. Not the most studied theologian.
Only the Father knows (Matthew 24:36).

That's why Jesus doesn't suggest occasional awareness —
He **commands continual vigilance**.
Not a casual glance heavenward now and again,
but a lifestyle of spiritual alertness.

This isn't about **watching the sky** every night,
but about **walking with Christ** every day.
Not about paranoia, but **purpose**.
Not panic, but **preparedness**.

It's not like revising the night before an exam.
This is more like **training for a marathon** —
You don't get fit the day before the race.
You prepare every day, steadily, so you're ready
when the starting gun goes off.

The call is for a steady heart, not a sudden scramble.
Jesus isn't after a burst of spiritual performance.
He wants **ongoing surrender**.

It's daily choices.
Daily prayers.
Daily repentance.
Daily love.
Daily obedience — even when no one's watching.

Imagine a soldier waiting on call. He doesn't sit around in pyjamas hoping for a late alert.
He sleeps in uniform, boots near the bed, gear packed.
Why? Because the command to move could come **at any moment**.

Jesus is calling us to that same spiritual posture — not sleepwalking through life,
but ready, watchful, alert in heart and action.

"Blessed is the one the Master finds doing His will when He returns." (Luke 12:43)

So this is not about waiting passively, like someone on a park bench checking the sky.

It's about **working faithfully**, like someone preparing for a guest they long to see.

He's coming — so live like it.

Illustration: Don't Wait Until It's Too Late

You don't wait until your house has been burgled to install a security system.
You prepare in advance — because the risk is real.

In the same way, don't wait until Jesus appears in the clouds to get your heart right.
By then, it will be **too late**.

It's like arriving at the port **after** the cruise ship has already set sail.
You're standing there on the dock —
Bermuda shorts on, Hawaiian shirt ironed, suitcase in one hand,
and the finest pair of Crocs you own proudly strapped to your feet...

You *look* ready.
You're *dressed* for the journey.
You've got all the gear.

But if you're not **on board**,
you're **not going**.

So many today look spiritually prepared —
they know the worship songs, share Bible verses on Instagram,
even have a favourite preacher.

But their hearts remain untouched by grace,
unanchored in surrender,
unmoved by the presence of Christ.

It's not about appearances — it's about **abiding**.

You can't fake a boarding pass when the trumpet sounds.
You're either on the Ark, or you're not.

Today's World: The Illusion of Time

In our culture of constant distractions and convenient delays, the idea of living ready for Jesus' return can sound... extreme. Outdated. Even a bit dramatic.
We are conditioned to believe that there's always more time — another day, another season, another chance.

So we put off the eternal for the sake of the temporary.

We tell ourselves:

- *"I'll surrender later — maybe when I'm older."*

- *"I've got time. I'm still figuring things out."*

- *"Let me sort my life out first — then I'll focus on God."*

But the most dangerous word in the enemy's vocabulary is **"tomorrow."**

Satan doesn't have to convince you that Jesus isn't real.
He just has to convince you that you've got **plenty of time** to decide.

We plan ahead for everything else:

- We set up pensions years before retirement.

- We pay into life insurance "just in case."

- We book holidays months in advance.

- We prepare for job interviews, weddings, even the weather.

But **the only event that's guaranteed to happen** — the return of Christ —
is the one thing most people push to the back of their minds.

We treat the coming of Jesus like it's a vague rumour rather than a **divine reality**.
We're ready for everything... except **eternity**.

But the truth is — **Jesus won't wait for us to get our priorities straight.**
When the moment comes, it will come suddenly.
Instantly. Without a second's delay.
No alarm. No countdown. No time to pack a bag.

If you're not spiritually awake now, you won't have time to wake up later.

This isn't about guilt — it's about grace.
Jesus doesn't call us to panic — He calls us to prepare.

The Urgency of the Hour

This is not a drill.
This isn't a sermon filler, a scare tactic, or a dramatic metaphor.
It's reality. It's Scripture. It's coming.

Jesus isn't just coming eventually — He is coming suddenly.

Not in a slow build-up with headlines and hashtags,
but in a divine instant — unannounced, unstoppable, unmistakable.

When the trumpet sounds:

- There's no **snooze button** to buy you five more minutes.

- No **text message alert** to give you a heads-up.

- No **grace period** to get your affairs in order.

It will be the most **sudden interruption** in human history —
and only those who are already ready will go with Him.

This won't be a time to start preparing — it'll be the moment your preparation is tested.

If you're waiting for a sign — this is it.

- Wake up from spiritual autopilot.

- Lock in your focus on what truly matters.

- Live holy — not perfectly, but surrendered.

- Get right with God — now, not later.

Don't fall for the lie that you'll have time to "sort it all out" one day.
One day is not guaranteed.

We spend our lives getting ready for things that may never happen —
weddings, house moves, job promotions —
yet we delay preparing for the one event that's promised in Scripture and confirmed by every prophetic sign:
The return of Jesus.

You don't need fear.
You need **faithful urgency** — a seriousness in

your soul that says,
"If He came today, I'm ready."

Live with your lamp full of oil.
Keep your spiritual bags packed.
Be found watching, not wandering.

Because when He comes,
it won't be to warn —
it will be to gather.

Keep Watch. Live Ready. Eternity Doesn't Wait.

Jesus' words weren't meant to frighten you —
they were meant to **awaken you**.
Not to cause panic, but to provoke preparation.
Not to scare you into religion, but to stir you into relationship.

He's not coming for the most polished,
the ones with the perfect past, the cleanest record, or the longest prayers.
He is coming for the prepared.
For the ones whose hearts are aligned with His.
For the surrendered, not just the successful.

And **readiness doesn't begin with your performance** —

it begins with your **posture**.
Not your résumé of good works,
but your heart bowed in faith.

This is not about religion.
It's not about ticking spiritual boxes or keeping up appearances.
It's about a genuine walk with Jesus —
real, raw, daily, and surrendered.

So **keep watch**.
Not with anxious eyes, but with expectant hearts.

Stay faithful —
not because you fear being left behind,
but because you long to be with the One who went ahead.

This is a love story, not a horror story.

You're not watching the skies for a stranger —
you're waiting for your Bridegroom.

And when He comes —
because He will come —
you don't want to be scrambling to get your spiritual life together,
making promises, confessing last-minute prayers,
or scrolling for answers.

You want to be ready —
found loving, worshipping, living, and walking with Him.

Because eternity doesn't wait.
And neither will He.

When the trumpet sounds,
He will come for those who are already His.

So don't delay.
Don't drift.

Choose readiness today —
because tomorrow may be too late.

Chapter 13

Faithful or Foolish — What Will He Find You Doing?

"Who then is the faithful and wise servant, whom the master has put in charge of the servants in his household to give them their food at the proper time? It will be good for that servant whose master finds him doing so when he returns. Truly I tell you, he will put him in charge of all his possessions." — *Matthew 24:45–47*

In these verses, Jesus shifts our attention from **when** He is returning to **what kind of people** He's returning for.

The focus moves from speculation to character — from timelines to trustworthiness.

It's not enough to simply keep one eye on the sky, waiting for His arrival.
Jesus wants to find His people **working**, **serving**, and **living faithfully**, as though He were already present in the room.

This servant isn't driven by emotion, convenience, or applause — he's anchored in **devotion**.
He doesn't grow weary in the waiting or slack off because of the delay.
He doesn't waste time trying to calculate the Master's return.
He simply stays ready by staying **faithful**.

Jesus is teaching us something vital here:
It's not the date that matters most — it's the state of your heart when He comes.

This is a test of **integrity**. And integrity is best measured in **obscurity**:
When no one's looking.
When there's no applause.
When you could get away with doing less — but choose to stay committed anyway.

Illustration: Faithfulness Behind the Scenes

Imagine an employee left in charge of a family business while the owner is away.
The lazy worker clocks in late, checks social media behind the till, and treats the shop like it's

a break room — assuming he has time to tidy up before the boss walks in.

But the **faithful employee** doesn't take chances.
He runs the place like the owner is watching through the CCTV — or better yet, like the owner could walk through the door at **any second**.
He isn't driven by fear of being caught out, but by a desire to honour the trust placed in him.

Or picture a soldier standing guard through the night.
Even if there's no threat in sight, and the world around him sleeps,
he stays alert — not because danger is certain,
but because his **loyalty is not conditional on visibility**.

Today's World: Private Faith in a Public Age

We live in a culture that values performance, platforms, and being seen.

Social media constantly rewards us for visibility
—
likes, views, validation.

But **kingdom faithfulness isn't about what's public — it's about what's done in secret**.

Some people live differently depending on who's watching:
one way in church, another way at home.
Holy in the pews, compromised in private.
They shine on Sunday, but fade by Monday.

But Jesus is not returning for part-time disciples.

He's not coming back for those who look good in Christian spaces,
but for those who live surrendered **when no one else is looking**.

Real faith isn't a spotlight moment — it's a **lifelong posture**.

It's the quiet prayers, the unseen acts of obedience,
the daily "yes" to God when compromise would be easier.

The Urgency of the Hour: Work While You Wait

Jesus is coming back. But when?

That's the point — **you don't know.**
No warning email. No 24-hour heads up.
Just the trumpet blast. Just the King, suddenly standing at the door.

And when He comes, He won't ask,
"Were you watching the signs?"
He'll ask, **"Were you faithful in the silence?"**

The reward Jesus offers is staggering:
the faithful servant will be entrusted with **more**
—

not because he was loud or gifted, but because he **served quietly and consistently**.

Don't live like the Master is delayed.
Live like He could return before you finish reading this chapter.

Because one day — He will.

So stay faithful.
Stay present.
Keep feeding the people around you.
Keep showing up to the assignment God has given you —

in your home, your work, your calling, your ministry.

Let Him find you **doing**, not just **dreaming**.
Let Him catch you **serving**, not just **scrolling**.
Let Him return to find you **faithful**, not just informed.

Faithfulness is the fruit of readiness.
And readiness is the posture of a servant who loves His Master more than His own comfort.

"But suppose that servant is wicked and says to himself, 'My master is staying away a long time,' and he then begins to beat his fellow servants and to eat and drink with drunkards. The master of that servant will come on a day when he does not expect him and at an hour he is not aware of. He will cut him to pieces and assign him a place with the hypocrites, where there will be weeping and gnashing of teeth."— Matthew 24:48–51

Jesus doesn't end this passage with comfort — He ends it with **a clear and sobering warning**.

The servant in question once held a trusted role. He knew the Master's will. He had been given responsibility. But what triggers his downfall?

Not open rebellion — but a dangerous assumption:

"My master is staying away a long time."

That belief is the seed of his destruction.
It dulls his conscience.
It erodes his reverence.
And soon, he slides from faithfulness into **entitlement**, then into **abuse**, **indulgence**, and outright **disobedience**.

He begins to exploit others, abandon his calling, and blend in with those who mock holiness.
Why?
Because he believes he has time.
He's convinced that judgment won't come — at least, not today.

But here's the truth:

Judgment does not delay simply because people delay repentance.

Sudden Return, Swift Reckoning

And then — without warning — the Master comes home.
No text message.
No alarm.
No final reminder.

Just **sudden arrival** and **swift justice**.

There's no time to clean up the mess, offer excuses, or pretend it didn't happen.
His fate is sealed. And Jesus doesn't mince words:

"He will cut him to pieces and assign him a place with the hypocrites..."

This is not symbolic slap-on-the-wrist language.
This is severe, final judgement.
This is **eternal separation**.

The servant is not merely punished — he is exposed as a fraud and placed among the hypocrites.
There, Jesus says, will be **"weeping and gnashing of teeth."**
A phrase that consistently describes **hell** — a place of **regret**, **agony**, and **no second chances**.

Illustration: The Classroom & The Shop

Imagine a student in a classroom.
The teacher steps out for five minutes.
One student decides: "Now the rules don't matter."

He throws paper, mocks classmates, trashes the room. He assumes he has time to cover his tracks.
But suddenly — the headteacher walks in.
The room freezes.
The chaos ends.
But **the judgement begins**.
What felt like harmless mischief now carries lasting consequences.

Or picture a trusted employee left to manage a high-street shop.
Thinking the boss won't be back for weeks, he starts stealing cash, throwing after-hours parties, mistreating staff.
Then, one night, the owner walks through the door unannounced.
The security alarm doesn't go off — but **justice does**.

Today's World: The Comfort of Delay

This parable is painfully relevant.

We live in a generation where **the fear of God has all but disappeared**.
Holiness is seen as outdated.
Morality is mocked.
Truth is twisted to fit preference.
And many say with confidence:

- "Jesus isn't coming back anytime soon."

- "It's been 2,000 years — probably just a myth."

- "If He was really coming, He'd have done it already."

This **false sense of delay** has made the Church sleepy and the world reckless.
People **trample grace**, **abuse positions of leadership**, and live as though eternity is a fairytale.

But let's be clear:

Jesus isn't slow — He's merciful.
His delay isn't denial — it's an opportunity. A window to repent.

168

But that window **will** close. And when it does, it will slam shut without warning.

The Urgency of the Hour

Jesus doesn't end this teaching with a hug.
He ends it with a hammer — a jolt to the complacent heart.

He's not calling for fans.
He's calling for **faithful stewards** — people who live like He could return before sunset.

He's not looking for half-hearted believers who act holy only when it's convenient.
He's returning for those who **take His Word seriously**, who honour Him in public and in private, who aren't lulled to sleep by the lullaby of delay.

The question is not **if** the Master will return.
It's **when**.
And when He does, your status won't save you — only your **faithfulness** will.

Conclusion and Final Warning

Jesus didn't teach Matthew 24 to spark **curiosity** —
He taught it to provoke **urgency**, inspire **faithfulness**, and **wake the complacent**.

This is not just a parable — it's a **mirror**.

Five scenes.
One message:

- Some will be taken; some left.

- Some are watching; some sleeping.

- Some are faithful; others faking.

- Some are waiting in reverence; others wasting time.

- Some will be rewarded; others judged.

What separates them?
Not church attendance.
Not how many Bible verses you know.
Not how religious you appeared.

It comes down to one thing:
Daily surrender. Faithful living. A heart

loyal to the Master — even when He feels far away.

You cannot afford to play church.
You cannot afford to delay repentance.
You will not receive a 15-minute warning before Christ appears in the clouds.
You won't get a countdown or a final sermon.
You'll get a trumpet.

And by then — it will be too late to start getting ready.

That Moment Is Coming

Perhaps today.
Perhaps tonight.

The sky will split.
The King will return.

Everything you believed — or chose not to believe — will become **unavoidable** reality.

And in that moment:

• There will be no more time to repent.

• No time to reconcile.

- No time to finally "get serious."

Only two things will matter:

1.   Did you truly know Him?

2.   Were you faithful in His absence?

The door is open now — but it won't stay open forever.

So don't gamble with eternity.
Don't assume you have tomorrow.
Don't wait for the "right time."

Be found ready. Be found faithful. Be found His.

Conclusion

The Final Wake-Up Call

So here we are — the end of the book.
And unlike your favourite Netflix series, this ending doesn't fade to black with credits.
No, this one ends with a trumpet.

We've journeyed through the powerful, prophetic words of Jesus in Matthew 24 —
through warnings, parables, comparisons, and deep spiritual truths.
From the days of Noah to the signs of the end,
from faithful servants to sudden raptures,
the message has been clear and unwavering:

Jesus is coming — and He's coming soon.

Not one prophecy has failed.
Not one word has expired.
The sky has not split yet — but it will.

The Days We're Living In

We are living in the generation that is watching Bible prophecy unfold before its very eyes.
A world filled with violence, corruption, deception, and pride.

A generation tampering with DNA, erasing God's design, and mocking His Word.
A Church — in many places — distracted by performance instead of presence,
focused on platform over preparation, style over surrender.

These are the days of Noah — again.
And once again, the Ark stands ready. **His name is Jesus.**

The Big Picture

Let's pause and remember what we've seen:

- We saw Noah's generation laugh at the idea of judgment — until the rain fell.

- We watched a world ignore the call to righteousness — until the door of the ark was shut.

- We examined our own generation — intoxicated by comfort, numb to urgency, asleep at the wheel.

- We heard Jesus' voice, urging His Church to **watch, be ready, stay faithful.**

Jesus doesn't just want us to **study** the end times —
He wants us to **live** like the end could come **at any time.**

He's not calling us to **panic** — but to **purpose.**
Not to **fear** — but to **faith.**
Not to **performance** — but to **surrender.**

More Than a Warning — This Is an Invitation

This book wasn't written to tickle curiosity or stir up debate about dates.
It was written as a final wake-up call.
To **shake** us from spiritual slumber.
To **clear the fog** of "someday" thinking.
To **compel a generation** to live like Jesus could return **today.**

And not just for yourself —

But for your family.
For your neighbours.
For your friends.
For your generation.

Because when He comes, it will be **sudden**.
When He comes, it will be **final**.
And when He comes — **only those in the Ark will be saved**.

The Ark Is Still Open

Now for the good news:

You still have time.
The door hasn't shut.
Mercy is still flowing.
Grace is still available.
The Cross is your ark.
Jesus is your only refuge.

You don't need to fix yourself first.
You don't need perfect theology or church attendance medals.
You just need a **humble heart**, a **surrendered will**, and a **genuine 'yes'** to the Saviour.

Romans 10:13 says:

"Everyone who calls on the name of the Lord will be saved."

Don't delay. Don't assume you'll have another chance.
You may not get a warning — just a trumpet.

Your "yes" to Jesus now is the only guarantee you'll ever get.

A Final Word to the Church

If you're a believer reading this:

Wake up. Lock in. Live holy.

This is not the hour to be casual.
Not the time to flirt with compromise.
Not the moment to blend in and hope no one notices your faith.

You were born for this moment.
You are part of the last generation before the return of the King.

So live like Noah:

- Walk with God when no one else does.

- Preach righteousness even when no one listens.

- Build the ark, even when they laugh.

- Stand firm when others compromise.

- Be ready when the trumpet sounds.

- When others drift, stay anchored.

- When others mock, keep building.

- When others wait, start warning.

Final Challenge: Be Found Faithful

There will come a day when everything stops.
The skies will split.
The Lord will descend.
The trumpet will sound.

And in that moment, **the only thing that will matter is this**:

Did you truly know Him — and were you ready when He came?

The runway is clear.
The passengers are boarding.
The flight is ready.

We're all seated aboard **Titus Airlines, Flight 777**, parked on the runway, waiting for air traffic control — **God the Father** —

to give the order to the pilot — **Jesus Christ** — "Son, go get Your Bride. You are cleared for take-off."

Let that be the moment you're found watching, not wandering.
Faithful, not faking.
Ready, not regretful.

The time is now.
The Ark is ready.
Get on board. Stay on board. And don't look back

Prayer of Commitment

Heavenly Father,
I come before You with an open heart.
I recognise the times we are living in — and I hear Your call to be ready.
No more excuses. No more delays. No more pretending.

I confess that I have sinned.
I've lived for myself. I've drifted. I've ignored Your voice.
But today — I turn to You.

I believe that Jesus Christ is the Son of God,
that He died on the Cross for my sins,
and that He rose again to give me new life.

I declare with my mouth: **Jesus is Lord.**
And I believe in my heart that God raised Him
from the dead.
So, according to Your Word — I am saved.

I step into the Ark of salvation — not by my
works, but by Your grace.
I give You my whole life — my past, my present,
my future.
I choose to follow You, to walk in obedience,
and to live as one who is ready for Your return.

Fill me with Your Spirit.
Cleanse me from within.
Keep me awake, watchful, and faithful
— until the day I see You face to face.

Thank You for saving me.
Thank You for loving me.
Thank You for calling me Yours.

In Jesus' name,
Amen.

Reflection Questions
Study Guide

Pause & Reflect

"As it was in the days of Noah, so it will be at the coming of the Son of Man." — Matthew 24:37

Take a few moments of silence. Ask the Holy Spirit to highlight anything in your life that's out of alignment with readiness. Be honest. Be humble. He already knows.

Questions for Reflection & Discussion

(Use personally, with a friend, or in a small group.)

Chapter 1: The Days of Noah — Then and Now

1. What stood out to you most from Jesus' comparison between Noah's generation and our own?

2. Which aspects of today's culture most remind you of "the days of Noah"?

3.   Have you ever experienced being mocked or misunderstood for your faith like Noah was?

4.   What does "walking blamelessly" look like in today's world?

5.   How do you personally guard your life against the spiritual and moral corruption that's becoming normalised?

Chapter 2: Corruption of Creation

6. How do modern technologies (CRISPR, AI, transhumanism) challenge or reinforce your understanding of God's design?

7. Do you believe the Church is prepared to confront the ethical and spiritual questions these developments raise?

8. What does it mean to protect and honour the image of God in a generation that seeks to redesign it?

Chapter 3: Noah Warned Them — But They Ignored Him

9. Why do you think so many people today dismiss the idea of Jesus returning?

10. What can you learn from Noah's persistence and faithfulness — even when it didn't make sense?

Chapter 4: The Gospel Is Our Ark

11. How does the imagery of Jesus as our ark shape your understanding of salvation?

12. Are there people in your life who need to "get in the ark"? How can you lovingly warn and invite them?

Chapter 5: The Door Will Close

13. What does living in "faithful urgency" look like day-to-day?

14. Are there areas in your life where you've assumed you'll "get right later"?

15. If Jesus returned tonight, would He find you watching — or drifting?

16. What distractions most often keep you from living with a sense of spiritual urgency? How can you practically refocus your priorities?

17. Jesus said, "Keep watch." What does that look like for you in your current season of life — as a parent, student, worker, or church member?

18. Are you more tempted to live like the faithful servant or the complacent one (Matthew 24:45–51)? What honest steps could help shift your posture?

19. When was the last time you genuinely longed for Jesus' return? What might be causing that longing to grow cold — or burn brighter?

20. If someone asked you how to "get in the Ark" today, how would you explain the gospel in your own words? Are you confident sharing it?

Space to journal

Use these prompts to write your thoughts or pray:

- Lord, help me stay awake and alert, even when the world is asleep...

- I confess I've been distracted by _____. Help me refocus on You.

- Holy Spirit, show me who in my life needs to hear the truth before it's too late.

- Jesus, I want to be ready — not with just knowledge, but with obedience and surrender.

Bonus Exercise: "If It Rained Today..."

Write a short letter as if you were Noah, speaking to this generation. What would you say? What would you warn? What would you invite them into?

Scripture Index & Key Verses

A quick reference guide to the Bible passages used and unpacked throughout this book.

✦ Matthew 24 – The Foundation Chapter

- **Matthew 24:3–8** – "The beginning of birth pains."

- **Matthew 24:12** – "Because of the increase of wickedness..."

- **Matthew 24:27** – "As lightning comes from the east..."

- **Matthew 24:36** – "No one knows the day or hour..."

- **Matthew 24:37–39** – "As it was in the days of Noah..."

- **Matthew 24:40–41** – "Two men will be in the field... one will be taken..."

- **Matthew 24:42** – "Keep watch, because you do not know..."

- **Matthew 24:44** – "So you also must be ready..."

- **Matthew 24:45–47** – "Who then is the faithful and wise servant?"

- **Matthew 24:48–51** – "But suppose that servant is wicked..."

✦ **Genesis 6–7 – The Days of Noah**

- **Genesis 6:1–5** – "The sons of God saw that the daughters of humans were beautiful..."

- **Genesis 6:9** – "Noah was a righteous man, blameless among the people..."

- **Genesis 6:12** – "God saw how corrupt the earth had become..."

- **Genesis 7:16** – "Then the LORD shut him in."

✦ **1 Peter 3:20–21**

- "...God waited patiently in the days of Noah... This water symbolises baptism..."

✦ 2 Timothy 3:1–5

- "There will be terrible times in the last days... lovers of themselves, lovers of money..."

✦ Luke 17:26–27

- "Just as it was in the days of Noah, so also will it be in the days of the Son of Man..."

✦ Romans 10:9

- "If you declare with your mouth, 'Jesus is Lord' and believe in your heart..."

✦ Romans 13:11

- "The hour has already come for you to wake up from your slumber..."

✦ 2 Corinthians 6:2

- "Now is the time of God's favour, now is the day of salvation."

✦ 1 Thessalonians 4:16–17

- "For the Lord himself will come down from heaven... we will be caught up together..."

✦ Jude 1:6–7

- "The angels who did not keep their positions of authority..."

✦ Genesis 3:5

- "You will be like God..." — Satan's original deception.

Sources & References

This book draws from Scripture, biblical scholarship, and contemporary research. Below is a list of key sources referenced directly or indirectly throughout the chapters.

Scriptural References

All Bible quotations are taken from the **New International Version (NIV)** unless otherwise stated.
NIV © 1979, 1984, 2011 by Biblica, Inc.™ Used by permission. All rights reserved worldwide.

Theological & Biblical Commentary

- **Matthew Henry's Commentary on the Whole Bible**

- **NKJV Study Bible**

- **KJV Study Bible Notes**

- **David Guzik's Enduring Word Bible Commentary**

Historical & Cultural Context

- **"The Life and Times of Jesus the Messiah"** – Alfred Edersheim

- **"The Jewish Wedding Analogy in Eschatology"** – Various Messianic Jewish teachings

- **Jewish Virtual Library** (www.jewishvirtuallibrary.org)

Scientific & Cultural References

- **CRISPR Technology and Gene Editing** – NIH (National Institutes of Health), Nature, and Scientific American

- **Transhumanism & Bioethics** – World Economic Forum reports, Wired Magazine, and MIT Technology Review

- **DARPA Human Enhancement Projects** – U.S. Department of Defense Public Reports

- **Artificial Intelligence and Neural Implants** – Neuralink, Elon Musk

(company statements and research updates)

Illustrative & Creative Sources

- Personal anecdotes and analogies created by the author for teaching and devotional use.

- Cultural illustrations derived from modern Christian preaching, storytelling, and observation.

Other Books by David Hancox – Available on Amazon

Less Is More: Less of me, more of God!

A devotional journey drawing from the life and humility of **John the Baptist**, encouraging readers to embrace dependence on God and live with greater spiritual clarity.

Be Still: 31 Days of Inspiration

A month-long devotional designed to guide you into daily moments of pause, reflection, and encountering God's presence through scripture and prayer.

Dear Pastor: 31 Days of Encouragement

A devotional crafted to uplift clergy with daily reflections, prayers, and reminders of God's faithfulness in ministry.

Notes

Notes

Notes

Notes

Notes

Printed in Dunstable, United Kingdom